GLIMPSES of AUSTRALIAN BIRDLIFE

GLIMPSES
of
AUSTRALIAN BIRDLIFE

PETER SLATER
and SALLY ELMER
with RAOUL SLATER

First published in 2014 by New Holland Publishers Pty Ltd
London • Sydney • Auckland

The Chandlery, Unit 114, 50 Westminster Bridge Road, London SE1 7QY, UK
1/66 Gibbes Street, Chatswood, NSW 2067, Australia
218 Lake Road, Northcote, Auckland, New Zealand

www.newhollandpublishers.com

Copyright © 2014 New Holland Publishers Pty Ltd
Copyright © 2014 in text and images: Peter Slater and Sally Elmer

All rights reserved. No part of this publication may be reproduced, stored in a retrieval system or transmitted, in any form or by any means, electronic, mechanical, photocopying, recording or otherwise, without the prior written permission of the publishers and copyright holders.

A record of this book is held at the British Library and the National Library of Australia.

ISBN 978 1 92151 742 6

Managing Director: Fiona Schultz
Publisher: Alan Whiticker
Editor: Simon Papps
Designer: Peter Guo
Production Director: Olga Dementiev
Printer: Toppan Leefung Printing Ltd (China)

10 9 8 7 6 5 4 3 2 1
Keep up with New Holland Publishers on Facebook
www.facebook.com/NewHollandPublishers

A thirsty Western Bowerbird.

CONTENTS

Introduction	7	Small honeyeaters	70-71	Hardhead	130-131
Glimpses of Australian Birdlife	9	Plumed honeyeaters	72-73	Pacific Black Duck	132-135
Small bush birds: Passerines	17	Golden-backed Honeyeater	74-75	Dusky Moorhen	136-139
White-winged Fairy-wren	18-19	Brown honeyeaters	76-77	Black-fronted Dotterel	140-141
Emmott's Fairy-wren	20-21	Willie Wagtail	78-79	Dotterels	142-143
Variegated Fairy-wren	22-25	Golden-headed Cisticola	80-81	Red-capped Plover	144-145
Red-backed Fairy-wren	26-27	Chestnut-breasted Mannikin	82-83	Red-necked Avocet and Banded Stilt	146-147
Kalkadoon Grasswren	28-31	Zebra Finch	84-85	Great-billed Heron and Ibises	148-149
Dusky Grasswren	32-33	Finches	86-87	White-necked Heron	150-151
Orange Chat	34-35	Striated Pardalote	88-89	White-faced Heron	152-153
Crimson Chat	36-37	Spotted Pardalote	90-91	Large waterbirds	154-155
Gibberbird	38-39	Cinnamon Quail-thrush	92-93	Australian Pelican	156-159
Red-capped Robin	40-41	Ground Cuckoo-shrike	94-95	Little Black Cormorant	160-161
Eastern Yellow Robin	42-43	Australasian Pipit	96-97	Pied cormorants	162-163
Yellow-rumped Thornbill	44-45	White-browed Woodswallow	98-99	Gull-billed Tern	164-167
Small brown birds	46-47	Masked Woodswallow	100-101	Caspian Tern	168-169
Weebill	48-49	Black-faced Woodswallow	102-103	Gulls	170-171
Treecreepers	50-51	Pied birds	104-105	Australasian Grebe	172-173
Varied Sittella	52-53	Apostlebird	106-107	Large bush birds: Non-passerines	174-175
Swallows	54-55	Bowerbirds	108-109	Emu	176-177
Tree Martin	56-57	Spotted Bowerbird	110-115	Australian Bustard	178-179
Fairy Martin	58-61	Western Bowerbird	116-121	Wedge-tailed Eagle	180-181
Scarlet Honeyeater	62-63	Northern bowerbirds	122-123	Little Eagle	182-183
Honeyeaters	64-65	Satin Bowerbird	124-125	Small kites	184-185
Little Wattlebird	66-67	Waterbirds: Non-passerines	126-127	Spotted Harrier	186-187
Friarbirds	68-69	Black Swan	128-129	Whistling Kite	188-189
Brown Falcon	190-191				
Owls	192-193				
Frogmouth and Owlet-nightjar	194-195				
Diamond Dove	196-197				
Crested Pigeon	198-199				
Flock Bronzewing	200-201				
Spinifex Pigeon	202-203				
Brown Cuckoo-Dove	204-205				
Kingfishers	206-209				
Laughing Kookaburra	210-211				
Rainbow Bee-eater	212-213				
Quail	214-215				
Southern Stone-curlew	216-217				
Banded Lapwing	218-219				
Inland Dotterel	220-221				
Cuckoos	222-223				
Major Mitchell's Cockatoo	224-225				
Galah	226-229				
Budgerigar	230-231				
Australian Ringneck	232-233				
Varied Lorikeet	234-235				
The Photographs	236				
The Poems	237				
Index	238				

Dedicated to Frank Elmer
1936-2012

Acknowledgments

We are grateful to many friends for companionship, advice, criticism and understanding. Among them are: Steve Parish, Ray Garstone, Graeme Chapman, Michael Morcombe, Neville Male, Cyril Webster, Stanley Breeden, Kay Williams, John Warham, John Halse, Grant Squelch, Monty Shrader and the Lindgrens, Harpers, McCrums and Griffiths. Pat Slater was a constant source of inspiration until her death in 2003; she also put Peter into many a hide, and pulled him out hours later, exhausted but exultant.

The poem on page 139, *Where are the swans*, is by Russian poet Marina Tsvetaeva.

Brown Cuckoo-Dove photographed in the rainforest on 'The Block', Bellthorpe, Qld, where Frank spent so many happy days.

INTRODUCTION

the master potter
seeking perfect pieces threw
on the eighth day: birds

Some time in the 1940s I was given a small paperback book entitled *Glimpses of Australian Birdlife* by Robert Hall, published in 1906. It must have come, via a favourite aunty, from a secondhand bookshop because it was rather battered and foxed but I loved it anyway. I still have it, more battered, considerably more stained by time and almost falling to bits because I read it so often when I was a child with an incipient passion for birds. So when Sally and I sat down to select the pictures for this book 70 years later, I immediately decided on the same title, hoping that our photos would inspire some youngster in the same way that the original book had inspired me. And if some older reader feels the impulse to buy a digital camera with a tele-lens, I can guarantee hours of pleasant experiences mixed with inevitable disappointments. Between us, Sally and I have spent more than 100 years observing, painting and photographing Australian birds, yet there is the feeling we have had but a glimpse. Two lifetimes are just the beginning.

I remember Bill Eastman, an American photographer and artist who was working on a book about Australian kingfishers in 1968, saying he wished he had a camera with a very long telephoto lens that he could just poke out of the car window and take his pictures. My reply was "Where would be the fun in that?' But such cameras now exist, ones that can be held in the palm of one's hand and sporting tiny lenses that extend to the digital equivalent of 1000 mm or more, something undreamt of in Bill's day. Perhaps before too long it will be possible to buy a camera with wings to photograph soaring eagles. But I don't regret the days I spent sitting in hides with primitive cameras or lugging clumsy and heavy equipment through the bush. Some of the results are here, others were taken with the latest state-of-the-art digital cameras: I can't see a lot of difference.

Peter Slater

My first trip out west into the desert with Peter, and I've just started using a digital camera. My first time in a hide, with a male Spotted Bowerbird at his bower just three metres in front of me! His antics in trying to entice a female into the bower are such that at times it is hard not to laugh aloud – hissing and mewing, strutting, bowing, picking up his 'treasures' then tossing them towards her. An hour later I scramble out of the hide happy, and casually say that I captured them mating. Stunned silence, then Peter says "Ahhh.... Sally. Hardly anyone has managed that!" When I later look at my photos, I am dismayed at how far out of focus they are, and realize how much I need to learn what a camera can do. Fortunately, these new digital cameras can take hundreds of images and I delete all the bad ones. Because I paint, I am not worried too much about pin-sharp focus or branches in the way – I just try to capture lighting and bird shapes, colours and attitudes, always thinking my paint brush can put in the details. And now, so many years later, with thousands of photographs taken (some of them pin-sharp!) and thousands of kilometres travelled, our trips are still an absolute pleasure for me.

Unlike twitchers, whose delight is the number of birds seen in a day, or a year or a lifetime (and we are both in awe of their dedication), we prefer to concentrate for a few days or a week on one bird or a small group of birds. So we have sat hidden, watching terns and pelicans fishing in desert streams, tightly-packed flocks of bronzewings whirring in to drink, bowerbirds displaying, fairy-wrens and chats feeding chicks, eagles on dead kangaroos, grebes floating in magical reflections in desert gorges, grasswrens on rocky spinifex-clad hillsides, galahs squabbling... our glimpses of ever-fascinating birdlife.

Sally Elmer

GLIMPSES OF AUSTRALIAN BIRDLIFE

I stand and look at them long and long

Walt Whitman

When a bird takes to the air and feels the rush of wind in its wings, does it experience the same joy that fills my soul as I watch? Does the eagle rejoice in its mastery as it catches a thermal to join the gods aloft? What does the fledgling fairy-wren feel when it takes its first flight? Is its emotional reaction: 'This is what I was born to?' We'll never know until we are reincarnated as birds. But what I do know is that I was born with a passion for birds, not sentimental at all, more a visual hunger that I try to express in photographs and paintings. Many before me have felt the same things and marvelled at the variety and beauty of Australian birds, leaving their impressions for us to enjoy. Can you imagine how Willem de Vlamingh felt in 1697 when he saw Black Swans on what is now known as the Swan River; what were Sydney Parkinson's emotions on encountering a Red-tailed Black-cockatoo in 1770; or Georg (sic) Forster's when he beheld a White Goshawk in 1774; or John Gilbert's joy when he first saw a Paradise Parrot in 1844 – all birds hitherto undreamt of? My reaction is like theirs; each bird seen is a new delight.

In decades-old memory, I am sitting near the old bridge where a huge colony of Fairy Martins lives, a locust-like stream of birds flying past me with beaks full of mud or insects, pausing awhile to plaster mud nests or feed ever-ravenous chicks before leaving to gather the next load. Out to my right stretches Lake Bindegolly. The sky is black and threatening, the lake is dotted with hundreds of Black Swans, the water silver, dead calm before the storm – black sky, black swans sitting on black reflections in a silver mirror. The old wooden bridge is a much more appealing repository for the martins' bottle-shaped mud nests than the modern concrete structure that will replace it a dozen years hence. I am waiting for the falcon. It has a nest away over the hill, and every hour or so it arrives to sample the banquet. The storm is rolling closer, the air is still, only the sounds of martins fluttering by and their soft pleasant calls. Suddenly a thunderous roar of wings, desperate escalation of panicked churring as a thousand martins take to the air. Out of nowhere the hobby arrives and flicks up onto its favourite perch. It is a male, beautiful and sleek, burnished blue back, black cheeks and tawny breast. It settles, ruffles its feathers and hunches down to watch, one foot up, head turning from side to side as the swarms of birds make height. A minute passes. Two, then three, eternity ticking, head still swivelling. Suddenly, its gaze is fixed, concentrated on one particular bird. I look up but cannot see what the hobby has noticed. With a gaze a dozen times more acute than mine it has picked out among the flying hordes some slight imperfection, some impairment in one individual, or perhaps a youngster just out of the nest, still unsteady in the air. Long wings unfurl and in less than an eye-blink the falcon reaches maximum speed, heading for the unfortunate victim. I pray it is a sick bird, to be granted a swift release rather than a lingering demise from disease. Desperate attempts to evade: now other martins, secure in the knowledge that it is not their turn, harass the hobby, but it doesn't give up the agile pursuit. Finally, the inevitable strike, feathers float down and alight gently around me. The tiny falcon spreads its wings wide, reaches down and nips its victim behind the nape, the *coup de grace*, turns and heads off, martin loosely dangling, to its plucking perch a kilometre away where it will deplume its prey before delivering the body to its mate. She will eat some morsels then feed the rest to her chicks, satisfying them for an hour or so. The silver water turns grey, sudden riffles skitter across the surface, the storm arrives, the martins dive back under the bridge, I run to my car, the swans retract their necks and disappear behind a watery curtain as the deluge begins.

Green Catbird, one of the birds listed at Lamington National Park by Roy Wheeler on his epic 600-species quest.

Next day, on an island at the far end of the lake, we are setting up a hide at a huge nesting colony of swans, when a Black-breasted Buzzard appears, slowly soaring on high-v butterfly wings. So intent is it on the swans and their down-quilted nests that it is startled when it sights us and suddenly reverses course, nearly falling out of the sky, and hurries off over the hill into the hobbies' territory. We see the flicker of wings as the hobby pair rises up and from half a kilometre's distance we hear their furious kecking as they repeatedly dive-bomb the buzzard, driving it away from the nest and its precious contents. With the intruder gone they thrill us for too few moments with an exhilarating exhibition of synchronised high-speed aerobatics, sickle-wings splitting the silver sky, then the pair peels off over the hill back towards their nest tree. The male zooms up a thousand feet and heads away down the lake towards the bridge...

Before Pat and I were married we went to Fisher Island in Bass Strait with Del and Eric Lindgren to band muttonbirds. We rowed a dinghy the short distance from Flinders Island to Fisher, and were warned about the tides, as the next stop was South America. After sleeping during the day, we ran over the island at night catching muttonbirds, noting the number if a band was already attached, or putting one on if the legs were bare. We soon learnt how sharp their beaks were; muttonbirds have a nasty habit of getting a good grip then twisting back and forth. I still bear scars. One we caught about six times a night was numbered 20402. I remember the number because that is how many scars I acquired. Either this, or another bird we caught, later set a longevity record, something like 40 years. From Fisher we could see a small islet about a kilometre away that was covered with terns so we decided to row over to take photographs. Most of the birds were Crested Terns feeding large chicks but there were some smaller ones I now think were White-fronted Terns. Once we had our pictures we headed back and on the way stopped to fish. After a while Del noticed the tide was turning, starting to swirl past the boat. Remembering the warnings about the tides I started rowing but the dinghy wasn't moving. We began to panic; Eric took one oar, I took the other and we pulled like mad. Still not making headway – South America here we come. Then Pat said "Would it help if we pulled up the anchor?"

I met Sally Elmer in 1983 at the inaugural meeting of the newly-formed Queensland Wildlife Artists Society. She showed me a lovely painting of two kookaburras. At the time I was on a tight deadline to finish the illustrations for *A Field Guide to Australian Birds* and I was looking for a good artist to help. So I asked her how long it had taken to paint the kookaburras. Two days. I was painting seven birds a day at the time so didn't pursue the matter, especially as she already worked full-time at the Queensland Museum, and eventually asked Ruth Berry to help. Sally organized annual exhibitions for our small group of bird artist friends including Greg Postle and Brent Harvey, so we kept in touch. When Pat died in 2003 I sat around for a few years being useless: she left me with her computers and printers, so rather than throw them out I tried to find out how they worked. On hearing that Sally was interested in producing limited-edition prints of her paintings I offered the use of my equipment and we eventually turned out 24 editions. While we were working I mentioned that the colour reproduction of the field guide shifted further from the original paintings every time it was reprinted. Sally suggested a new edition. Over the next 12 months she rescanned all of my original plates, colour-corrected them, shifted birds around to accommodate the latest information, and also provided some paintings; that's her on the cover. During the course of the year we discovered that we had a mutual interest in deserts, so once the guide was finished we headed off to the Simpson Desert, and have spent a month or two each year since looking at others, such as the Tirari, Strzelecki, Pedirka, Tanami, Gibson and Sturt's Stony Deserts, concentrating on birds.

There are birdwatchers, like us, and there are twitchers who aim to see as many species as possible. The first real twitcher I met was Timothy Dixon, a lawyer who worked his way around the world looking at birds. He came to one of our bird meetings in Perth in 1957 and reported that he'd seen a Franklin's Gull on the foreshore at Bunbury. The Brass dismissed the idea; after all Franklin's lived thousands of miles away and was surely not possible in Australia, but after the meeting he told some of us more amenable enthusiasts that he was quite familiar with the species in America, and had twitched many other gulls as well so was able to eliminate them. Since when has a Silver Gull had a black head? Franklin's, of course, has been recorded quite a few times since, with photos to prove it, so I am convinced now, as I was then, that his identification was correct and that this constituted an Australian first. I met the other sort of twitcher shortly afterwards, a visitor from the eastern states and someone quite well known. He wanted to see a Western Shrike-tit, so I drove him about 200 kilometres down to Dryandra where I had recently seen some. When we pulled up the car, I heard a shrike-tit calling, and spotted it in the top of a Wandoo tree at a

Little Wattlebird calling, happy to share the garden.

Eastern Great Egret fishing.

distance of about a hundred metres, singing away, golden breast aglow. The famous birdwatcher raised binoculars for ten seconds, entered a tick in his notebook, got back in the car and we headed back home.

When we lived in Derby, WA, in the 1960s we were often visited by birdwatchers wanting to see the local specialities. The Holy Grail back then was the Black Grasswren, a bird that had only been recorded once before, when the Kimberley Medical Officer, Dr Frederick House, collected the new species while traveling with the Brockman Expedition, exploring the rugged north-west Kimberley in 1901. We spent a lot of time searching without success, mainly because we didn't do the obvious thing, namely to read the report of the expedition, which pin-pointed the locality where the original birds had been found. One party that contacted us consisted of Brigadier Hugh Officer, a legendary birdwatcher, and his mate, Max McGarvie from King Island, who was no slouch either. We headed off with high hopes and stopped at a likely spot. Max made a cup of tea. Now, Max doesn't use one pound of tea if two are available; you've probably heard it said that you can stand a spoon upright in a good bushman's cuppa – well you'd be battling to get a spoon into Max's. I took one sip and headed off behind a bush. When I'd recovered an hour or two later we marched off through the pindan towards a rugged pile of rocks that had the aspect of good grasswren territory. I was paired off with the Brig and he kept up a steady flow of conversation as I focused my eye on the rocks ahead. I spied some movement and turned to alert the Brig – he was a hundred metres away! Such was the carrying power of his parade-ground voice, honed to megaphonic perfection on the Indian North-west Frontier, that

I had thought he was still alongside me. Alas, we didn't find the grasswren but the Brig did ask me to illustrate his book on Robins and Flycatchers, a request that precipitated a career change from teacher to artist. We were able to show him some new birds including the Rufous-throated Honeyeater which he needed for his book on honeyeaters. When Pat and I travelled to Victoria, we stayed with the Brig at Olinda. We took him out to dine at an expensive-looking restaurant and he began to regale us with tales of his time with his Pathans in the Khyber Pass. Well, gradually a hush came over the restaurant as the diners listened spell-bound, knives and forks poised, as enthralled as we were. Once the talk returned to birds, meals were reluctantly resumed. When the Brig heard that we had named our son Raoul after the RAOU (Royal Australasian Ornithologists Union) he thereafter called him Boc after his beloved Bird Observers Club. As a youngster our son referred to himself as Raoul Moore Bocarini Slater, the only person in the world named after two birdwatching societies. Now that the two societies are amalgamated into one, Birds Australia, I've never heard Raoul call himself Ba.

Another legendary birdwatcher was Roy Wheeler, who ran the Bird Observers Club for many, many years. Monthly meetings he chaired had some of the fervour of religious revival congregations. He was one of those people loved by everyone and consequently had friends all over Australia, standing him in good stead when he undertook to be the first to see 600 species in on year. He made it, too, on the 31st December. Sean Dooley went a step further and logged 700, a prodigious feat that unbelievably has subsequently been exceeded. Sean's book *The Big Twitch*, detailing his travels, is a classic. When Roy retired he went to live at O'Reilly's Guest House in the Lamington National Park, introducing many visitors to birds in his inimitable fashion. Each year we joined him for the annual Bird Week which actually lasted for a fortnight. One day was set aside to see as many birds as possible and the first stop was a swamp. Roy sent young Raoul to run around the perimeter to flush snipe. It was productive work, because the master paid him two bob (20 cents) a snipe.

Elsey, Bishop of Kalgoorlie, was a friend of my father's and in 1948 he gave me a book on nature photography by the Kearton brothers, written in the early 1900s. They were pioneers in the use of hides to photograph birds, and I soon adopted their ideas. Even more than the ease with which photos could be taken was the absolute joy of being close to an unsuspecting wild creature behaving naturally. Eventually I decided that wool-bales made ideal hides, being the right size and easy to move closer in stages over a few days to gradually accustom the subjects to the new addition to their environment. So I went to the logical place to buy wool-bales, Elder Smith's headquarters in St Georges' Terrace, Perth. I asked at reception about buying wool-bales and was escorted to an office on the first floor. From there I proceeded floor by floor to offices of increasing opulence until I was sitting with the managing director at the top, overlooking a magnificent vista of the Swan River. A secretary took my order for tea, and we sat, the Director and I, discussing the prospects of the season, and I was thinking these guys really know how to look after their customers. When the Earl Grey arrived, the director asked me how many bales I required. "Three" I replied. Actually he took it quite well and I finished up with seven recycled bales from a

Masked Lapwings on the beach.

Black Kite waiting for the intruders to leave so that it can resume feeding.

dingy shed in the back streets of Fremantle, a gift from the wool-broking firm, with perhaps a hint not to return.

In 1955 I was working at the Kimberley Research Station when the Ord River flooded, rising to lap at my doorstep. Once the waters receded thousands of Barramundi headed upstream and we each caught dozens. That night there was a feast: the heads and entrails were dumped on the bank further downriver. Next day I noticed a large mixed flock of Black and Whistling Kites feeding on them, so set up a hide. I asked one of the farm-hands to put me into the hide, explaining that then they wouldn't know I was inside. So I arranged my camera, tripod and stool, and called to my assistant that I was set. Hours went by – several kites landed in nearby trees but showed no signs of venturing closer. I kept thinking: I'll give it another hour, surely they'll come. Then a voice from behind me said "They don't seem to be coming in, do they."

I was lucky enough to meet and learn from a great bird photographer of the black-and-white era, before the universal introduction of colour. John Warham, an Englishman, came to live in Australia and photograph birds, traveling around the country in a Blitz Wagon (which did one mile to the gallon) with a dark-room on the back. On many occasions I sat with him watching as the images magically appeared in the developing tray, lit by eerie red light. Digital photography makes it too easy; what is lost is the art and the mystique of producing perfect prints. John visited Eclipse Island near Albany, WA, studying and photographing the Little Shearwaters that nest there, sowing the seeds for his illustrious subsequent career. At the opposite corner of Australia, on Raine Island, he photographed a Herald Petrel at its nest, which was a new bird for Australia. From there he travelled to New Zealand, eventually being recognized as the world authority on seabirds. What impressed me most about the Warhams was the dedication of John's wife Pat, who worked behind the scenes and acted as 'go-awayster' at hides.

Some of my more cynical friends back in the sixties suggested that the reason I got married was to have a built-in 'go-awayster' in the shape of Pat, to put me into hides and walk away, theoretically fooling the birds that danger had gone, wander off to sit under a tree with a book for hours on end then return and drag me triumphantly into the light of day. Of course there was no truth in that at all. If there was, I repaid her many times over when she became an editor, author and internationally respected horse photographer. Anyway, many of the pictures in this book couldn't have been taken without her help, and I register here my heart-felt gratitude.

...It has become obvious over the years that many small bush bird species in drier woodlands are in decline. There are numerous factors at play but one of the most obvious is the proliferation of feral cats, followed by foxes and pigs. It is past time to forgo sentiment and introduce biological controls to eradicate them. Nevertheless there are still plenty of birds to enjoy and each time we venture into the bush we find new bird wonders. It is a privilege and a joy to watch, photograph and paint them. In return we try to be as unobtrusive as possible so they can go about their daily routines without interruption. These are our glimpses of Australian birds...

Many rails that live on islands lose the ability to fly; the Tasmanian Native-hen is a typical example. Unfortunately many species that evolved on small islands have become extinct following the introduction of feral predators.

Red-capped Robin.

SMALL BUSH BIRDS: *PASSERINES*

About half of the world's birds are classified as passerines. They are often called 'songbirds' and 'perching-birds'. Neither is a good description because many non-passerines 'perch' and many 'sing' (although in nearly all cases the songs are neither as melodious nor as varied as those of most passerines). To define a passerine in simple terms is not easy; most of their characteristics are internal, such as uniquely-structured spermatazoa, but there are many exceptions, so only a few visible features are common to *all* passerines and not found in other birds. One is the shape of the foot: three toes directed forward, without any webbing between them, and one backward, attached to the leg at the same level as the front toes. Non-passerines have a variety of different foot configurations, including webbing and reduced numbers of toes. Most passerines are small, but some such as lyrebirds are large. Hopefully the following photographs will help sort out in the minds-eye of an observer new to birdwatching which sorts of birds are passerines and which are not. Does it matter? It's a first step in learning what birds are about.

WHITE-WINGED FAIRY-WREN

Basically an arid-country bird, the White-winged Fairy-wren favours low shrubbery such as salt-bush, blue-bush, eremophilas, cassias and spinifex, and is a common denizen of the sand dunes of the centre. Like other fairy-wrens it moves in family parties, consisting of mainly brown birds. Most of the groups we have seen have been attended by only one fully-plumaged male. We often find their nests and I can't recall any occasion where more than one coloured male helped in feeding the chicks. When other males intrude into a territory, the resident performs a spectacular display with raised feathers and waggling tail. The shot on the left of such a display was taken within sight of Uluru, NT. The moulting male on the right was on a sand dune, also near Uluru. We saw it on *Grevillea pteridifolia* flower-heads, presumably searching for ants rather than nectar. The female (above) is the plainest of the female fairy-wrens, with only a hint of blue in the tail.

EMMOTT'S FAIRY-WREN

Probably the greatest honour any mortal can achieve is to be commemorated in a bird's name. Worthy individuals like David Fleay (*Aquila audax fleayi* – the Tasmanian Wedge-tailed Eagle), H G Barnard (*Barnardius zonarius* – the Australian Ringneck), Rev J B Love and Edwin Ashby (*Ashbyia lovensis* – the Gibberbird) are among those so immortalised. Add to the list Angus Emmott who has a race of one of Australia's most beautiful birds named after him and his family, *Malurus splendens emmottorum*. I photographed this pair just south of the Emmott property in western Queensland; at the time I didn't realise I was looking at a newly described subspecies of the Splendid Fairy-wren. Such is the breadth of Angus's knowledge of wildlife, he could probably identify the insects the fairy-wrens brought to the nest for their chicks as well as the plants the nest was built in.

VARIEGATED FAIRY-WREN

In the east the Variegated Fairy-wren is not as intensely pigmented as the populations further west, yet it is still spectacular in its own way. Any patch of bushland, particularly where there is lantana for cover, will provide a home for a tightly-knit group of up to six or eight birds, often including two or three fully plumaged males. One such family party shares Sally's property in the mountains near Maleny in Queensland and accept her as part of their world. She took these photos as the wrens went about their daily routines rearing their chicks and ignoring her completely. Above is one of the three attendant males carrying a dropping away from a nest containing two chicks. It is also shown on the right displaying with quivering wings to the female. Another male is pictured on the left. Both of these males have the entire head blue; a third younger male with a grey patch in the crown occasionally attended the nest as well.

VARIEGATED FAIRY-WREN

The wren on the right was one of three males feeding two chicks. While the other two fed and left in a matter of seconds, this male often took a break after feeding the chicks and sat comfortably relaxed on a nearby perch for up to five minutes, not at all worried by Sally standing just two metres away. The morsels brought to the nest included march-flies, small grasshoppers, small dragonflies, spiders, caterpillars and moths. Juicy items like the spider above provide adequate hydration. On the left is the female; she spent a lot of time brooding the chicks to keep them warm, and as a result her tail was bent, due to the confines of the domed nest.

admire these bush gems
but don't get too close to them:
just don't get bitten

RED-BACKED FAIRY-WREN

Male fairy-wrens regularly invade neighbouring territories and attempt to mate with the dominant female. Often the invading male will carry a whole or partial flower petal in the beak. The male on the right is holding a fragment of a red milkweed flower petal. DNA analysis has shown that such an inducement to mate is often successful, thus strengthening the gene pool. On the right is a female carrying a grass stem to incorporate into her nest. She was very busy, adding another piece of grass every 3.8 minutes for about 20 minutes, then taking a rest to feed. Although there were two other females in this family group, we didn't see either assisting in the construction of the nest; later we did see them helping to feed the chicks, as did the male.

KALKADOON GRASSWREN

We spent a lot of time on the rocky spinifex-clad slopes in north-west Queensland looking without success for this elusive grasswren. Then on the morning we were due to leave I got up early and drove to a likely-looking hillside. I emerged from the car as the first rays of sunlight were burnishing the spinifex seed-heads, took two steps, looked up and there they were, sunning themselves on a rock ten metres away. I've seen nearly every Australian bird, but the thrill of seeing one of the few remaining is still the same as it was when seeing my first. The birds were so intent on soaking up the sun's warmth after a freezing night that they allowed a close approach. When I had some shots I raced back to camp to pick up Sally, returned and found the wrens still on the rock: my shots of males are to the left and right, Sally's female is above. The following year when we returned the hillside was burnt, ash blowing in the wind, with stark black sticks as headstones for lost sprites.

THE GRASSWREN AND THE ROCK-WALLABY

The rocky spinifex-clad hillsides in north-west Queensland are favoured by the Purple-necked Rock-wallaby as well as the Kalkadoon Grasswren. After finding stark fire-ravaged hillsides where we had seen them the year before, we located both in an untouched patch near Dajarra and spent many pleasant hours in their company. The grasswrens were much harder to observe because they mostly kept to the spinifex, but occasionally came out onto the rocks. We didn't realise at the time that this was the precise locality where the rock-wallaby was discovered and described in 1924 by Albert Le Souef, uncle of my beloved biology teacher, Mildred Le Souef Manning. The grasswren is named after the Kalkadoon people who inhabited the area and were massacred on Battle Mountain. The tragic story, the grasswrens and the locality inspired me to write a poem:

kalkadoon spirits
flit among the spinifex
on battle mountain

DUSKY GRASSWREN

One of my most vivid memories of a trip through the Macdonnell Ranges in 1974 was of spinifex-clad hillslopes back-lit in the late afternoon sunshine with tantalising glimpses of Dusky Grasswrens. When we returned 30 years later I was looking forward to similar experiences. Alas, the hillsides for kilometre after kilometre had been burnt, with only pockets of spinifex remaining. We checked out some of the more likely looking spots, and found grasswrens in three of them, usually only a few birds, slight evidence to suggest that those in the burnt areas hadn't survived. On one rock outcrop, densely grassed with old spinifex, we stumbled on a pair with a nest and shared some magical hours with them as they busily gathered grasshoppers for their chicks. The male is on the left, and the female above and to the right.

ORANGE CHAT

The male on the left was the first Orange Chat I saw, spied on a samphire bush on the floodplain of the Gascoyne River. I was so taken by the brilliant plumage that I followed, losing sight as it went to ground, then picking it up again as it flew up onto another bush 50 metres away. Thus we made our way for about a kilometre until, on its latest reappearance, it held a caterpillar in its beak. When it flew down into a samphire I realised it had a nest. The bird, having observed me following without incident, must have decided I was no threat, and over the next hour or two arrived with food for the three large chicks, ignoring me so I was able to take this photo with my hand-held camera from about a metre away. The female was equally trusting. The pair above was photographed 55 years later on a wind-blown day in the Simpson Desert.

CRIMSON CHAT

Peter and I were watching a male chat at Kilcowera Station in Queensland when a female arrived with a moth in her beak. She approached the male, offering the morsel which her mate took, then he flew down to their nearby nest and fed the chicks. This is the only time we have seen a female of any species giving food to a male – usually it is the other way around. The female wasn't concerned by our presence and fed the chicks herself every few minutes when the male wasn't present. One hot September day near Coober Pedy, SA, we watched a pair of chats feeding their nearly-fledged chicks in a desert bush on a rocky hilside. The three chicks were prodigiously voracious – in a period of two and a quarter hours around midday the female arrived with food 42 times and the male came 22 times – 64 visits in total with grasshoppers, caterpillars and spiders, or one every 2.1 minutes. The male seemed to be partial to spiders and his throat-feathers were matted with spider-webs. Examining our photographs later we noted that on many occasions more than one insect was held in the beak, so it is probable that nearly 200 invertebrates were fed to the chicks in the short time we were there. The nest was in a low isolated bush on a seemingly barren desert hillside, so the ability of the diligent parents to find succulent morsels so easily truly astounded us.

37

GIBBERBIRD

Gibbers are stony desert plains, at first sight lifeless, soulless places with shimmering horizons and pitiless skies. But pause and look closer – there is birdlife here: pipits, larks, pratincoles, dotterels and, best of all, Gibberbirds, which are found nowhere else. They feed on seeds and insects; in our limited experience, the main items are grasshoppers, themselves adapted to the gibbers, looking like pebbles. Although male and female have bright yellow underparts, they are surprisingly difficult to spot. After rain the gibber-plains blossom and their inhabitants breed while good conditions last. We found this nest after seeing a bird run across the road carrying a beakful of nesting material. From a distance we watched it building under a small prickly bush for a week or so; it became accustomed to our presence so, when it eventually laid and began incubating, we were able to take its picture peeping out from the bulky nest. Being only a few metres from a dirt road, the nest was subjected to a cloud of dust every few minutes as another cattle-train passed by. We wondered why the bird, with a million hectares of gibbers to choose from, had decided on that spot. At no stage did we see a male in the vicinity; he might have suggested a better place, but still left the female to do all the work.

RED-CAPPED ROBIN

Wherever we camp in mulga or gidgea woodland we find Red-capped Robins. In one particular favourite campsite near Cunnamula, Qld, we found, in the 1970s, 15 pairs in an area of about ten hectares. Over the years fewer pairs were detected and on our last visit in 2009, following a long period of drought, we could only find one pair. They were attending a nest which had been destroyed when we checked a fortnight later. However, in many other sites where we have camped they are still common. Younger females (right) have grey foreheads; older females (above) acquire a reddish forehead and very old females get a pinkish blush on the breast as well.

EASTERN YELLOW ROBIN

The scientific name of the yellow robins is *Eopsaltria* which means 'dawn-singer', a much more appropriate name than 'robin'. First of the bush birds to start calling, well before day-break, these birds have no relationship with the true robins of the northern hemisphere and should by rights be called by another name. One day someone will think of something. They are quiet and confiding in the bush and are one of the easiest bird families to photograph. I find it surprising that a bird which goes to some trouble to camouflage its nest then sits on it with its glowing yellow breast in full view. The Western Yellow Robin has a grey breast, making it much harder to detect the female when she is incubating her eggs. Which has the better success rate? Possibly if there was more predator pressure in the west this factor has led to a loss of colour on the breast.

*yellow robins call
before the kookaburras'
welcome to the dawn*

each time it calls 'chip'
seven hundred times a day
another tree falls

YELLOW-RUMPED THORNBILL

In Manjimup, WA, where I spent my tender years, we called these perky little birds 'chip-chips' after their calls. I can remember following them in our backyard as they jerkily nid-nodded their way over the lawn. When I got too close they would fly up into the lucerne tree, then seem to fall backwards on the perch before righting themselves. I couldn't understand why they did that. Still can't. Years later we lived for a while in an orchard where numerous thornbills seemed to survive the persistent spraying by our landlord. One pair nested near our house and over a period of months built four bulky untidy nests, but in each case something caused them to abandon construction. Then the pair started work in earnest at a new site, frantically adding material until the nest was a metre long, so heavy that it too fell down. They moved closer to the house, built again as if they had just been practising, laid three eggs and at last reared some chicks. I set up my camera and took the shot on the right as a tribute to their persistence.

SMALL BROWN BIRDS

The first Southern Whiteface I photographed had a nest in a metal down-pipe near our home in Kalgoorlie. Subsequently I have come across nests in farm sheds, old tractors and fenceposts, but most have been in more typical situations, built in a tree-hollow, preferably with a knot-hole entrance. Most individuals are very plainly coloured, but some we have come across have buff underparts, exciting the unwary into thinking they have stumbled upon the extremely rare Chestnut-breasted Whiteface. Sharing its arid habitat are the sweet-singing Redthroat (above) and the two wedgebill species, which are very similar in appearance, looking like the Chirruping (left), but have very different incessant songs.

WEEBILLS NEST-BUILDING

While we were enjoying the natural sculptures of the Devil's Marbles we stumbled across a pair of Weebills adding to their almost-completed nest being constructed at eye-level in a small eucalypt. They were remarkably tame so we spent a couple of days watching them. We are pretty sure only two birds were in attendance – at most of the other Weebill nests we have found, three or more birds were cooperating. Other Weebills did fly into the tree while we were there, but they were driven away with much vociferous swearing. Weebills are very vocal and this pair was no exception. To take the picture on the left Sally positioned herself so one of the 'marbles' was in the background. We kept a note of their arrival times and they averaged one visit every seven minutes for about an hour then were absent for 20 minutes or so before resuming their busy schedule. The items carried in were often quite large and would easily be noted by alert cuckoos, particularly the Horsfield's Bronze-Cuckoo which often perched nearby.

49

TREECREEPERS

Australian treecreepers obtain their food either on the ground or on the trunks and branches of rough-barked trees, where they spiral upwards. They appear to be unable to turn around and move head-first down the trunk. I once watched a treecreeper at a waterhole with fairly steep banks – it didn't seem to know how to descend to the water and eventually rather hesitantly backed down. The colours of different species roughly reflect the bark colour of their favoured trees. These pictures were all taken at the entrances to nest-holes; Rufous Treecreeper of the south-west (left); Black-tailed Treecreeper of the tropics (far left); Brown Treecreeper of the east (above); and White-browed Treecreeper of the inland acacia woodlands (right). We observed the latter bringing many empty pupal cases of Caper White butterflies to the nest cavity. When we checked, we found the nest and eggs were blanketed in them.

VARIED SITTELLA

Whereas treecreepers are most comfortable working their way up treetrunks, sittellas can move in any direction, even upside-down along the underside of branches. They are usually observed in small closely-knit groups of up to half a dozen individuals. Males have a dark cap (above); females have the entire head black with an obvious yellow eye-ring. The nest is a neat masterpiece, built in an upright tree-fork. In our study area in south-west Queensland, the nest is invariably situated in a Leopardwood tree (left and right). The name 'Varied' refers to the five different forms that inhabit Australia. Those in the south have orange windows in the wings, just visible in the bird to the left; in the north the windows are white, as seen above. Where the different forms come into contact they hybridise – the nesting bird shown here on the right is a hybrid between the orange-winged form of the south-east and the black-capped form of the south-west.

SWALLOWS

Aerial mozzie-zappers, swallows appear to have fared pretty well from human changes to the environment. Welcome Swallows (above and right) are common around human habitations, building their mud nests under eaves. White-backed Swallows tend to feed higher in the air than other swallows and have a more fluttering, almost bat-like flight, but dig their nesting tunnels in vertical sand-banks. In the arid inland, roadway cuttings are favoured sites, like those in these photos (an adult on the left and a juvenile on the right). This young one was photographed leaving the nest-tunnel – it was one of half a dozen chicks. Once they leave the nest they fly strongly for a while with their parents then line up behind them like a train to return to the tunnel for a rest. One of my favourite birding delights is watching the train of youngsters flying at speed about a metre apart, popping one after the other into the burrow, pop, pop, pop, pop. I'm still waiting for a pile-up.

TREE MARTIN

The only real difference between martins and swallows is in the shape of the outer tail-feathers – rounded in martins and elongated in swallows. Tree Martins nest in tree-hollows, usually with a horizontal entrance (right) so they can fly straight in. At Mootwingee, NSW, we located a nest in a vertical hollow, the only one we've seen (left). To fly into the hollow the martins dived in head-first from above. We've occasionally seen Tree Martins bringing wisps of grass as well as beakfuls of mud to line the nest-cavity, but usually eggs are laid onto bare wood-dust.

FAIRY MARTIN

Most Fairy Martins now nest under man-made structures but a substantial number still utilise natural sites such as overhanging rock faces and tree trunks. While we were camped on Gilmour Creek near Birdsville, Qld, we took the opportunity to watch a large colony building under a massive eucalypt branch overhanging the creek. They had chosen to build within metres of a popular campsite so were accustomed to human presence – in fact they ignored humans completely and we were able to sit in comfort on the riverbank and marvel at the busy activities. One of my favourite compositional devices, rarely achieved, is a single point of stillness in a blur of activity, Quite by accident I managed such a shot (opposite) when a martin hovered near its nest, beak full of mud pellets, with only its head still as it rapidly beat its wings while others hurried by.

SQUATTERS AND THIEVES

While we were watching the Fairy Martins on Gilmour Creek actively building their nests, we noted a number of small domestic dramas. The bird on the left kept trying to enter the nest it is shown clinging to, despite the efforts of the rightful owners to drive it away. It appeared to be hoping to take over an almost completed structure to save itself the considerable effort needed to make one of its own. The bird on the right was stealing mud from a nest under construction, also to avoid having to fly down the creek to the nearest mud-patch. It too was often driven away but kept returning for another beak-full. The following year a massive flood washed the nests away – a few pairs relocated further down the creek when the water subsided, but still built below the flood-level, due to the scarcity of suitable sites. The bird above was inspecting the tree trunk for a possible nest site.

SCARLET HONEYEATER

We look forward each year to the blossoming of eucalypts in the forest near home because there is a chance that Scarlet Honeyeaters will arrive. Some years they are present in hundreds, and when they are sated with eucalypts, visit our garden for a sip of evodia, grevillea and callistemon nectar for variety. Once several pairs even nested in our backyard. In other years there are hardly any even though the flowering seems to be the same. For many years I maintained a small waterhole in the forest with a hide nearby, taking water down every day. If the Scarlets were present they were the most persistent visitors (left). On one very hot day I counted 13 fully coloured males at the water's edge at the same time. I risked a photo but such are their reflexes that, following the noise of the mirror flipping up, there were only four visible by the time the shutter fired.

fiery red-head
thinks: two bees or not two bees
that is the answer

HONEYEATERS

One of my prized possessions is a hand-coloured engraving of Lewin's Honeyeater by John Lewin himself. When he illustrated it in 1808 he called it the Yellow-eared Honey-sucker. It wasn't until 1837, long after he died, that it was named after him. On the left is a Lewin's Honeyeater front-on showing the effect of an awesome mouth due to the yellow gape and ear-patch, an illusion no doubt of benefit to such an aggressive species. Above is a close-up showing pollen on the forehead – such honeyeaters are important pollinators of a wide variety of plants. A similar but smaller bird is the Yellow-spotted Honeyeater (right), once known as the Lesser Lewin. It has a longer, finer bill, a differently shaped ear-patch and is confined to north Queensland. We managed to snap this bird arriving at its nest with a beakful of nesting material less than a hundred metres from the northernmost tip of Cape York.

LITTLE WATTLEBIRD

The Little Wattlebird is a common visitor to gardens planted with native banksias, grevilleas and callistemons. Noisy and aggressive, it is constantly chasing and harassing competitors for the nectar-rich flowers. It is an important pollinator and frequently has a dusting of pollen on the forehead. You may wonder why a bird called a wattlebird doesn't have any wattles. The reason is that its larger relatives, like the widespread Red Wattlebird and the Yellow Wattlebird from Tasmania, do, a case of the lesser suffering for the skins of the greater.

FRIARBIRDS

Do friars nowadays still have bald pates? Probably not, but in times past they did, for no reason that I can imagine (although Sally suspects it has something to do with halos). So when a large vociferous bald honeyeater was discovered it seemed only natural that it should be called 'friarbird'. There are a number of species but the Noisy (left and right) is the most bald-pated. All of them are noisy but this one is more so – I recall watching a nesting pair when a Brown Falcon flew past; the friarbirds took off after it, yelling furiously, chasing it for at least a kilometre. In flowering trees and shrubs they are very aggressive, warning competitors off with loud cackling and raised hackles (left). They also seem to have long conversations with a limitless vocabulary. What are they gossiping about? That is a serious question; to us it sounds as if they are communicating in a way few other birds do. Above is the Little Friarbird, equally garrulous, but more sedately tonsured.

SMALL HONEYEATERS

The Painted Honeyeater (left), uttering its loud *Georg-ee* call, we photographed in the Simpson Desert, surprising to us because we normally see them further east in mulga country. It is a neat- looking bird but I find its bill rather unattractive; evolution though has a different aesthetic, for the beak is ideally suited to handling mistletoe berries, which are its principal item of diet. The other birds are White-plumed Honeyeater (far left) at Cooper Creek, Qld; female Banded Honeyeater (above) photographed in a loose nesting colony in the Kimberley, WA; and male Black Honeyeater (right) nesting in a hop-bush in western Queensland. The tiny male has an extraordinarily penetrating call, a single *pee-eep* which is audible over several hundred metres.

PLUMED HONEYEATERS

Over the years the common names of many Australian birds have changed, sometimes more than once, but we now have a general consensus of opinion as to those that are most appropriate. The idea of having a standard set of names is so that everyone knows which bird is being referred to. Most names are entirely appropriate, for example the Grey-headed Honeyeater (left and above) which clearly has a grey head. But the Grey-fronted Honeyeater (right) needs some clarification to explain its name. It comes down to what is meant by 'front'. One would expect it to refer to the breast and abdomen, but these parts are clearly not grey in the image. The 'front' in a bird is the area above the beak, analogous to the forehead in humans. In the case of this bird the grey front area is a few millimetres wide, or at least it is on individuals in the south of the bird's distribution, but this feature is lacking further north, as in this bird from Tennant Creek, NT, which lowered its head to make the point. Is it an appropriate name or not? It doesn't really matter as long as everyone uses it.

busy thrip-gleaner
hanging there by its toe-tips:
heavy golden back

GOLDEN-BACKED HONEYEATER

I came across a Golden-backed Honeyeater's nest (far left) by following one of its builders after it stole some nesting material from a Rufous-throated Honeyeater's nest I was watching. At that time this subspecies of the Black-chinned Honeyeater had only been observed nesting once before, so I built a rickety bush-tower to take some pictures. The nest was attended by five birds; all proved remarkably tame. John Hutchinson called to see us at Derby and mentioned that he wanted to take up recording birdsongs. We took him out to the nest and he set up his very bulky equipment on the tower. I have a photo of John holding his microphone about 30 centimetres from one of the obliging birds while it sang. I can guarantee that it was the easiest recording he ever made, He of course went on to become one of Australia's best in this demanding and difficult field of endeavour. The other two photos, taken at Camooweal in north-western Queensland, illustrate the bird's acrobatic ability in gleaning thrips from eucalypt leaves.

BROWN HONEYEATERS

A number of Australian birds have 'brown' in their names – Brown Booby, Brown Quail, Brown Falcon, Brown-backed Honeyeater, Brown Cuckoo-dove and Brown Songlark. Yet in none of these birds is the brown colour the same, varying from deep chocolate in the Brown Booby and anything from sooty-black to rusty-red in the Brown Falcon. The colour of the Brown Honeyeater (above) is closer to Ridgeway's olive-citrine, so perhaps we should think of it as Brown's Honeyeater after its discoverer Robert Brown, a botanist and naturalist who sailed with Matthew Flinders. To the right is one of the smallest members of the family, a female Black Honeyeater. Left is the Rufous-banded Honeyeater, which appears to us to be 'browner' than the Brown Honeyeater.

WILLIE WAGTAIL

It may seem strange to say that the Willie Wagtail is not a wagtail, but a large fantail. True wagtails feed on the ground, wag their tails up and down like their relatives the pipits, and breed in the northern hemisphere, migrating in small numbers to Australia. Willie Wagtails wag their tails from side to side, take most of their insect food in the air and are resident here. The bird on the left was feeding on midges in a wet year on Eyre Creek in the Simpson Desert. It turned up while we were sitting, hoping for bronzewings to arrive to drink, a typical example of 'wait-and-see' photography. Along the road verges in the desert we often see wagtails perched on well-dead kangaroo road-kill, catching flies, and also collecting fur to line their nests. Above is a hungry chick photographed closer to home in Sally's shade-house.

GOLDEN-HEADED CISTICOLA

In what passes for lawn at our place cisticolas often build their nests – these are two that I found after seeing the females carrying thistle-down into clumps of longer grass. The nest itself is protected by leaves actually *sewn* around the outside using the sharp beak as a needle and spiderweb as thread; the male has been observed sewing the outer leaves as well as the female. While watching the female feeding her brood I am constantly amazed at the size of the culinary items she forces down their throats. I've never seen a male attend a nest with food but other observers have. Cisticolas moult twice a year; in winter the male loses its golden head-colouring and in both sexes the tail is substantially longer than in summer.

CHESTNUT-BREASTED MANNIKIN

Mannikins are finches with heavy beaks well suited to seeding grasses. While I worked at the research station on the Ord River in the east Kimberley, WA, in the 1950s, I noticed that some Chestnut-breasted Mannikins were inter-breeding with Yellow-rumped Mannikins, a bird with similar shape and habits but with plain plumage. Numbers of Yellow-rumps had markings that appeared to be acquired from Chestnut-breasted genes. Some of the nests I found were used by both species. In the normal course of events these two would keep separate but at the research station experimental plots of rice and sugar cane provided an ideal habitat that suited both, and they often flocked together. A finch breeder, Noel Ives, told me that after a number of generations, 13 if I remember correctly, his supposedly pure Yellow-rumps produced a Chestnut-breasted. Or was it the other way around – I can't remember? My verse refers to the Russian poet Marina Tsvetaeva, who penned the lovely line '*Your name is a finch held in my hand*,' and to her suicide in 1941.

tsvetaeva died
holding a finch in her hand
so sad a passing

ZEBRA FINCH

After a series of good years in the inland regions, Zebra finches breed up in such numbers that for a while they are probably our most numerous species. They exploit the prickly thorn-bush, an introduced pest shrub from Africa that proliferates in the interior. Up to a dozen nests may be found in one bush, used for roosting as well as breeding. They also frequently use tree hollows (right). After rain, males begin their courtship displays, holding grass stems in the beak (left). Drought conditions hit them hard and numbers plummet. Nevertheless Zebra Finches are popular aviary birds, mainly overseas, and dozens of colour varieties are bred; it wouldn't surprise me to hear that, including all of these aviary birds, the Zeb is the world's most abundant passerine. It and the non-passerine Budgerigar could be Australia's two biggest gifts to international aviculture.

double-barred finches
busily checking their armpits
for body odour

FINCHES

When we moved into our home on acreage on the outskirts of Brisbane 40 years ago, Double-bars (left and upper right) often nested in our backyard alongside Red-browed Finches (lower right), Chestnut-breasted Mannikins, Spice Finches, European Goldfinches and House Sparrows. It's many years now since we have noted any here; the last three appear to have vanished altogether from our district, no great loss as they are introduced species (although I quite like goldfinches), but they epitomise a worrying trend. On a wider scale a number of finches are vanishing: the southern race of the Star Finch has virtually disappeared, the Black-throated Finch too is going from its southern range and the chocolate form from south-eastern Queensland is extinct in the wild. The Gouldian Finch reached crisis point but appears to be recovering slightly in some areas. What is to blame? It is easy to point the finger at changes in fire regimes following the dispossession of the original inhabitants, and the subsequent change from native to introduced grasses. In the case of the Gouldian, trapping for aviculture was probably a factor. In the 1950s I was told there were 40 licensed trappers operating in the Kimberley; Dr Eric Lindgren and I actually saw 7,000 Gouldians in the holding-cages of one trapper in 1956, all due for export. The other birds pictured here, the Plum-headed Finch (far right, above) and the Painted Finch (far right, below) are more secure for now.

STRIATED PARDALOTE

There are a number of distinct races of the Striated Pardalote. To the left is an example of the black-headed race from south-eastern Queensland, attacking its reflection in a car window. An example of the western race (above right) and its mate dug their nesting burrow in soil holding the roots of a dead tree. Much of the nesting material they carried consisted of strips of bark.

On the right is the yellow-rumped race from Derby in WA. These birds commonly dig their tunnels in heaped roadside verges – we counted 27 flying out of burrows as we slowly drove along a 15-kilometre bush track that ran north to south; most of the burrows were on the eastern side of the track. This race and the black-headed nest in winter over much of their range.

SPOTTED PARDALOTE

A twitcher from overseas described the Spotted Pardalote as Australia's best-kept secret. Certainly it deserves a high ranking among the world's beautiful birds. For me to say it is one of my favourites means nothing because whatever bird I am looking at, whether Peregrine Falcon or sparrow, is my favourite at that moment. But there is something special about this tiny jewel. Living and feeding among leafy tree-tops for most of the year, it comes down to ground-level to dig a burrow, with seemingly inadequate excavation equipment, to house its cup-shaped nest. A number of times I have noticed a tell-tale bare patch on the trunk of a particular species of stringy-barked eucalypt, waited a few minutes and seen a pardalote arrive to strip a beakful of bark for its nest, returning for another load every few minutes. Male (left) and female (right) share nesting duties.

CINNAMON QUAIL-THRUSH

As a youngster I never paused to wonder how quail-thrushes got their name until I flushed one near Kalgoorlie, WA. It startled me with the loud clatter of wings like a quail and I had a sudden revelation: "So that's it!" Since then I've had a special affection for them, particularly the ones that live in the desert, and I've tramped many a rocky hillside in the hope of a glimpse. How can they survive in such a seemingly hostile environment? Okay, after rain the desert blooms and insects abound but what about the years when there is no rainfall. The hardiest manage to hang on somehow and breed when the good times come, passing on their painfully acquired genes for survival. They nest on the ground, usually under an overhanging rock or a fallen branch. My friend, Monty Shrader, showed me how he made suitable nest-sites by scraping a small depression in the ground then constructing a tepee of three or four sticks over the scrape. It worked surprisingly often On the left is a female and above and right a male.

GROUND CUCKOO-SHRIKE

When I was aged about ten or so a friend lent me his binoculars. Only one eye-piece functioned and the magnification was only three times, but I set off on my bike with a zinging heart. The very first bird I saw through the single eye-piece was a Ground Cuckoo-shrike, naturally enough walking on the ground. Because I could see the black wing I thought it was a Black-shouldered Kite, the first of many misidentifications that led me eventually to produce a field guide to birds. So it is a sentimental favourite. Seventy years later Sally and I pulled up under a gidgee tree to camp, south of Coober Pedy, SA, unaware that a pair of cuckoo-shrikes was nesting above. They soon made their presence known; luckily they ignored us and we spent two days watching them. Both adults were feeding their chicks at regular intervals, mainly on grasshoppers, averaging one visit with food every 6.4 minutes, or about 70 times a day. At the change-over, when the one arriving was about 20 metres away, it always called and the brooding bird responded and left.

AUSTRALASIAN PIPIT

One of our most widespread birds, the pipit was the 15th most common species recorded by the 3,000 participants in the 1984 *Atlas of Australian Birds*, but didn't make the top 40 in the 2003 *New Atlas*. On our travels it doesn't seem to be any less abundant, but recently a well-travelled observer asked me if I had noticed a decline in pipit numbers; obviously he had. We have photographed it in our backyard near Brisbane, Qld, and in extreme deserts in the centre. The colour of pipits more or less reflects the soil where they live, being darker in more humid areas like the south-western bird on the left at Woodanilling, WA, and paler in the desert like the cinnamon example on the right which was photographed at Cacoory in far-western Queensland. In two of these shots the very long claw on the hind toe is clearly visible.

WHITE-BROWED WOODSWALLOW

Whenever we come across these woodswallows on our travels in the outback we stop because they are a good indicator of productive areas; often we will find accompanying honeyeaters like the Pied and Black as well as chats, cuckoos and finches. There is a constant stream of woodswallows soaring at height over the inland searching for a patch of woodland that has received good rain with its attendant proliferation of insect life and flowering plants. There they will stay a while and breed if the conditions are good enough. Twice I have been camped in a 'good spot' when woodswallows arrived and within a day or two started to examine likely nest sites: on one of those occasions near Cunnamulla, Qld, some pairs had eggs within a week. These photos indicate typical nesting sites; most are within two metres of the ground. Males (left, right and far right) and females (above) share nesting duties.

MASKED WOODSWALLOW

Flocks of White-browed Woodswallows in the east often contain lesser numbers of Masked Woodswallows; in the west the position is reversed. The two are closely related and do hybridise. At Cacoory near Birdsville we found a nest where the female was a hybrid and the male was a Masked. The nest contained chicks so, at least in that instance, the hybrid was fertile. Unfortunately a sparrowhawk put paid to our hopes of a photo, the only time I have ever cursed a sparrowhawk, a bird I dearly love. There were about a hundred nesting pairs in the vicinity and in the three weeks we were there the sparrowhawk didn't take any more, so why did it have to choose that one? The nest pictured here was in a typical site on a fallen branch about 50 centimetres from the ground. The bird to the right was feasting in a blossoming bloodwood tree – both woodswallows delight in the nectar-rich flowers and have a honeyeater-like brush tongue to take full advantage.

BLACK-FACED WOODSWALLOW

Many birds of the arid inland don't have a regular breeding season but rather nest in response to rain. Among the first to respond are Black-faced Woodswallows. My mentor, Dr Dom Serventy, often used to say that if a cloud obscured the sun they would start nest-building. A slight exaggeration, but on several occasions we have witnessed woodswallows starting to build their nests the day after it had rained. In the Simpson Desert we photographed the bird (above and right) picking up twigs and adding them to a nest site in the morning after heavy rain had fallen during the night. Woodswallows in general have several interesting features: as far as I know they are the only small passerines that have powder-down feathers, resulting in their soft appearance; and they are the only small passerines that habitually soar. Another feature is their habit of clustering at night and in cold weather (far left).

PIED BIRDS

Both of these species live in my backyard. I am constantly aware of the Magpie-lark because the female of my resident pair attacks her reflection in the window of my studio a dozen times a day. As soon as I start my mower (which is not as often as I should), Pied Butcherbirds arrive to feast on insects, frogs and lizards revealed by the scything blades. However, in each case the pictures here were taken in central Australia, the Magpie-lark (left) in the Macdonnell Ranges and the Pied Butcherbird at the Devil's Marbles. Both are common throughout Australia but, surprisingly, in Tasmania the butcherbird is absent and the Magpie-lark is rare.

APOSTLEBIRD

For the past 40 years a party of Apostlebirds has shared our backyard. They nest twice a year but their numbers haven't changed much, varying from seven to 13, occasionally numbering 12 'apostles'. Two or three times a year a bigger mob arrives and a very noisy interaction ensues. Sometimes one of them stays and joins our group permanently and sometimes one or two of ours leave. Where we live is quite the wrong habitat for Apostlebirds so I suspect that they are descended from aviary birds that either escaped or were released. When we throw out birdseed they fly down to feed, preferring oats; they often hold down a grain with one foot while pecking at it. While they are close we can detect their strong smell, which probably assists their bonding, as they spend a lot of time clustered together with mutual preening. Despite the fact that we have willing subjects close to home, we took these pictures at a mud nest in Bladensberg National Park near Winton in central Queensland.

BOWERBIRDS

Most birds are monogamous, a condition where a male and a female form a bond for breeding, but a considerable number have other arrangements. Some are polygamous, either polyandrous (female with multiple mates) as in button-quail or polygynous (male with multiple mates) as in birds of paradise and bowerbirds. Males of some polygynous species gather together on display grounds known as leks where visiting females make a choice presumably based on the most flamboyant display. There are two sorts of leks, one where all the males gather in one spot and the other where males are spread out, usually within earshot of each other. In the case of bowerbirds the display grounds are more widely spread, not necessarily within hearing range, but females are aware of their locations and probably visit all in their area before making a choice to mate, probably dictated by the ornamentation at the bower and the effectiveness of the displays. There are several sorts of bowers: avenues like the Satin Bowerbird's bower (opposite) and the Western Bowerbird's (above); maypoles like the Golden Bowerbird's bower and courts like the Tooth-billed Bowerbird's leaf-strewn arena. Young males regularly visit bowers as well, learning techniques to be utilised when they build their own. Most avenue bowers are oriented north to south with most ornamentation at the northern end. The female usually enters from the south, but once while we were watching this bower (above), the female arrived at the northern end.

SPOTTED BOWERBIRD

The Spotted Bowerbird inhabits drier woodlands over the eastern half of the continent, its place being taken in the west by the similar Western Bowerbird. We have come across the bowers mostly in mulga or calitris woodlands, often under the drooping skirts of Wilga trees, but also under fallen branches. The outer walls of the bowers are usually thin twigs while the interior is lined with dried grass stems. In the centre is a little heap of ornaments that appear to be particularly favoured. At the northern end of the bower is a collection of ornaments, mostly sheep-bones, pebbles, glass, fruit and in this case seed-pods of the endangered *Acacia ammophila* and a gecko skin (right).

SPOTTED BOWERBIRD

When a female arrives she enters the bower from the southern end where she can judge from the arrangement of ornaments viewed through the avenue walls and from the vigour of his display whether or not to mate with a particular male. At the height of a display the male's nuchal crest is raised and the feathers separate into discrete units (left). On nearly all of the occasions we have witnessed, the visiting female made the decision to leave through the northern end without consummation (right).

SPOTTED BOWERBIRD

The time and effort put into building and maintaining the bower and its surrounds is only possible because there is a plentiful supply of food, so the male doesn't have to spend much time feeding. In most cases we have observed, the male fed largely on wilga seeds. These photos illustrate aspects of the male's display, including wing-quivering and tail-fanning. At a different bower, Sally captured a successful culmination of all the hard work (right).

WESTERN BOWERBIRD

F T Gregory collected the first known specimen of the Western Bowerbird in 1861 on his expedition to the north-west and forwarded it to John Gould without any particulars. Gould noted its similarity to the Spotted Bowerbird and named the new species *guttata*, also meaning 'spotted'. The specimen didn't have the beautiful lilac nape so was apparently immature. Shortly afterwards J M Stuart, newly returned to Britain from his epic journey through the centre of Australia, gave Gould a bowerbird head he had collected, including the nape. In the 1869 *Supplement to the Birds of Australia* two Western Bowerbirds arebeautifully illustrated (above); for the upper bird the artist H C Richter must have combined the body of Gregory's specimen with the head from Stuart; the lower bird, in a similar posture to the left-hand photo, is probably entirely based on Gregory's immature specimen.

WESTERN BOWERBIRD

The focal point of the builder's territory, the bower, where we spent a week observing, was oriented north to south under a large spreading Rock Fig and was built on an extensive platform of sticks, substantially bigger than the platform laid by the Spotted Bowerbird. The male spent a lot of time placing twigs and grass stems in the bower walls and re-arranging the decorations that surrounded the avenue; most were at the northern end and there was a small heap of prized possessions inside the bower. Usually visits were for five to ten minutes, but once we recorded activities over a period of almost an hour. Inside the bower the male 'painted' individual grass-stems with material held in the beak (upper left), mostly after fossicking in the sticks at the south end of the platform. We couldn't see what was being picked up but at other times we saw an over-ripe fig and possibly an ant being used (lower left). Other bowerbirds (mainly young males) visited the bower and one in particular rearranged decorations and even 'painted'. Green weeds that grew around the fig tree were regularly harvested and carried to the bower. Usually the male hopped over to the weed patch and spent some time selecting a leaf that suited him (right) then hopped back; the weed patch was to the south so most of the leaves were deposited at the southern end of the bower. In the week that we were there an area of about three metres square was mowed.

WESTERN BOWERBIRD

Bowerbird displays at and around the bower are performed with vigour and elan, and these are not rendered satisfactorily in the frozen instants of still photography. Thus the 'wing-flicking' on the left occurs so quickly that we weren't aware how far the wings extended until the shots were examined later. In most of our photos of this display the head was obscured in the entrance of the avenue. The activity above and on the right, which we called 'attacking the bower', surprised us as we hadn't seen its like at Spotted or Satin Bowerbird leks and we couldn't imagine what function it could have. It recurred several times with the bird hitting the wall with extended feet; these are Sally's shots as she has the instantaneous reflexes necessary to capture such a fleeting instant. There was no attempt to dismantle the bower so it is unlikely that this was a rival male.

NORTHERN BOWERBIRDS

To me there is something reptilian about the Great Bowerbird (left) and I suspect it looks much like a post-apocalyptic feathered dinosaur without the teeth. I feel sure that some of those survivors of the giant meteor strike at the end of the Cretaceous period hopped rather than ran, just like the Great Bowerbird moving around its display ground. In the photo (left) the male bird looks as if it is interacting with the photographer but it is actually presenting its nape towards the bower, while uttering is characteristic hiss (is that the sound small dinosaurs made?). The Fawn-breasted Bowerbird (right) lives northwards from about Coen on Cape York Peninsula and in New Guinea as well; this arena was very close to the tip of Cape York (less than 1 kilometre). The half-dozen or so bowers I have seen were built on substantial platforms, no doubt because of inundation during the wet season. It differs from the other Australian avenue-builders by draping ornamentation on the walls. The hide at this bower was full of mosquitoes – our friend Michael who used it after us acquired Ross River Fever following a day-long session.

SATIN BOWERBIRD

Bowerbirds are ideal subjects for study, as much of the year's activities can be observed at one spot and such aids as video-cameras and voice-activated recorders can be utilised. The Satin Bowerbird has probably been studied more than any other. I remember spending time with Rita Vellenga, one of the early researchers, and found her vast knowledge enthralling. Our very superficial involvement is confined to just watching and taking the odd shot. On the left, a male is presenting a yellow leaf in a bowing display; we have noted a build-up during a display cycle, starting with a blue object, then yellow and finally a cicada nymph exo-skeleton. Raoul photographed an unusual 'double bower' (right). The male is shown 'painting'; after a shower of rain an immature bird arrived and painted the same twigs.

WATERBIRDS : *NON-PASSERINES*

Waterbirds are non-passerines that include distinctive assemblages like herons, cormorants, pelicans, rails and grebes. Australia is reputedly the driest continent, but there are many species that rely on water, from seabirds to shorebirds and ducks.

BLACK SWAN

The sight of swans that were black, not white, must have bewildered Captain Willem de Vlamingh when he first saw them on the Zwaanenrivier (Swan River) early in 1697, just another strange encounter in a strange 'new' land. Their blackness reminds me of spine-chilling lines from a poem by the Russian poet Marina Tsvetaeva:

—*Where are the swans?*
—*They went away, the swans.*
—*The ravens too?*
—*They stayed behind, the ravens.*

But their blackness is an illusion; underneath is a white swan trying to get out – just check their wings when they take off. I mention later (on page 219) the evocative sounds of Banded Lapwings flying over at night when I was very small. The other sound I recall from early childhood was the lovely soft bugling of Black Swans heading over our home for some distant waterway. The memory inspires a poem:

wild bugles blowing
dark shadows obscure the moon:
black swans overhead

HARDHEAD

J D Macdonald in his well-researched book *The Illustrated Dictionary of Australian Birds* states that the name 'Hardhead' is of uncertain origin. I suspect it comes from duck-shooters to explain why they consistently fail to hit it in flight, claiming that shot-gun pellets bounce off rather than conceding that this fast flier is too quick for them. Maybe the wide white flash in the wings upsets their aim. I hope so. In earlier days we knew it as the White-eyed Duck, but there are a number of almost identical waterfowl in other countries also with white eyes (in the male only) so to be consistent it would have to be the Australasian White-eyed Duck which is a mouthful, hence Hardhead, the shooters' name. Perhaps other countries should follow suit, then we would have Australasian, Ferruginous, Baer's and Madagascan Hardheads. It would be interesting to know if hunters find those other species equally hard to hit.

PACIFIC BLACK DUCK

"Water off a duck's back" is a cliche actually meaning something else, but ducks do have waterproof feathers, due to their tightly interlocking barbules. Underneath the feathers is a dense layer of down that traps air, enabling ducks to float high in the water. Cormorants, and darters in particular, have less down and float lower in the water; they are also more efficient in swimming underwater. To bathe ducks have to flap vigorously to wet the down (above) and afterwards spend a lot of time preening, spreading oil from the uropygial gland onto the feathers.

PACIFIC BLACK DUCK

Almost every park in Australia that includes expanses of water has a population of Pacific Black Ducks. The birds become so habituated to hand-outs that they lose their innate fear and could almost be considered domesticated. But in wetlands away from civilisation they are difficult to approach, taking off at any sign of disturbance. It is well known from banding studies that they are great travellers, so many of these 'tame' birds probably join the wild flocks. Do they immediately become 'wild' themselves? I can't recall ever coming across tame birds on any outback lakes or rivers. Pacific Black Ducks interbreed with Mallard. A northern hemisphere species that was introduced into Australia, indicating that the relationship between species is very close despite their very different appearance. Above is a female hybrid with a chick – such birds can usually be identified by their orange legs.

DUSKY MOORHEN

Public gardens with ornamental lakes are attractive to moorhens, and because of the over-supply of handouts from kindly humans there is generally an over-population. As the breeding season approaches territorial disputes over limited territory are frequent. The physical clash between these two birds is probably not typical of behaviour in natural situations where disputes are more symbolic. In this instance the argument continued for a few minutes and was watched by a ring of half a dozen birds; at least one, possibly a mate, joined in the fray (above) when the rival being attacked was vigorously submerged.

DUSKY MOORHEN

These are such attractive birds that I feel sorry they are so easy to see in ornamental parks. One should have to work harder to get a glimpse, like Lewin's Rail, which is one of the most difficult.

BLACK-FRONTED DOTTEREL

Any stretch of fresh water with a sandy or muddy margin anywhere in Australia is likely to attract at least one pair of Black-fronted Dotterels. Wherever we are camped in the outback it is not unusual to hear dotterels flying over at night, searching for reflected star-light on dams, creeks, ponds and water-holes. If more than one pair arrives they stake a claim to part of the shoreline. Where two territories abut there are likely to be confrontations that in our limited experience are more noisy than physical (left). These photos were taken in deserts after heavy rain. All of the nests of the Black-fronted Dotterel that we have found, save one, were a considerable way from the nearest water. The exception was a nest pointed out by my father on his last visit; it was doubly-atypical, being a metre from a salty creek at Gulugaba, Qld. Above is a chick we saw near the bore drain on the huge Bilpa Morea claypan in western Queensland.

DOTTERELS

Both of these dotterels, the Red-kneed (left and above) and the Black-fronted (right), seem to prefer freshwater on the inland waterways. Indeed the former is said to lack a salt-excreting gland. This gland filters excess salt from the bodies of birds like seabirds, gulls and cormorants that live in marine environments. The excess salt is excreted in droplets of concetrated liquid through the beak. While I was photographing a Red-kneed at a nest on a salt lake in Western Australia, I was interested to note the typical saline droplets forming on the beak-tip, so if it doesn't possess a gland, it must have some other mechanism to cope with salt when it occasionally visits salt lakes. The Red-kneed Dotterel always looks to me as if it is front-heavy and about to topple forwards.

RED-CAPPED PLOVER

This diminutive plover is much more partial to saltwater habitats than the similarly-sized Black-fronted Dotterel, which only occasionally ventures onto saline wetlands. The Red-capped is common in arid environments; we found the male (above) and the immature (left) on a bore-drain at Mitta Mitta on the Birdsville track. It also favours marine beaches and mudflats; the bird (right) with an egg and a just-hatched chick chose to nest a metre or so above the high-tide mark on the mangrove mudflats at Derby, WA. Note how well the chick's downy plumage matches the surroundings.

RED-NECKED AVOCET
and
BANDED STILT

When I was young the only books on birds I had access to were written by Alec Chisholm, and from these I gained the impression that nobody knew where Banded Stilts nested. So when I saw some on Rottnest Island, I was convinced I was about to make history, not being aware that a breeding colony had been found on an island in a salt lake in South Australia and another at Lake Grace in Western Australia. I ran all over the island, unfortunately without success. In 1964 Graham Pizzey, Eric Lindgren and I hired a plane to fly over Lake Grace, hoping to find them breeding. Later the pilot told me he didn't think the plane was going to make it over the trees at the end of the bush airfield, due to our combined weight, in which case there would have been fewer Autralian field guides in years to come. We did make it, just, and flew over the lake. I was in the back with the spare tyre, naturally, and spotted a huge flotilla of stilts. "There they are," I yelled and the pilot banked so suddenly I nearly fell out. After that I shut up. Anyway the stilts weren't nesting, just feeding. Since then colonies, sometimes of thousands, have been located on inland salt lakes. One of the mysteries of bird behaviour is how the stilts become aware that a lake somewhere out in the desert fills and explodes with sufficient brine-shrimp to support a colony, and how birds from scattered localities around the periphery of Australia head off and find that one lake. Above is a mixed group of Banded Stilts and avocets on a salt lake in South Australia. Red-necked Avocets either nest alone or in much looser, much smaller colonies. I photographed the nest opposite at Lake Biddy, near Lake Grace. My hide was close to the water and I watched avocets and stilts catching brine-shrimps a few metres away, marvelling at how neatly they juggled the crustaceans in their long bills.

GREAT-BILLED HERON AND IBISES

Because they return to swamps and reedy lakes to breed, we think of ibises as waterbirds, but much of their foraging occurs on dry land, often far from water. The beak is probably very sensitive because they are able to find crickets in burrows in grass-covered paddocks and extract them easily after delicate probing. They often fly in flocks, wheeling down in unison after sighting likely-looking grasshopper and caterpillar havens. The Australian White Ibis (above) has almost reached pest status around parks and gardens, so the species is probably not fully appreciated. Not all Straw-necked Ibises display full iridescence; to see an individual like the one opposite is usually a combination of age, freshly-moulted feathers and the best angle of viewing. The Great-billed Heron (left) is confined to coastal mangroves and creeks from Burma to northern Australia. We have had instances of keen twitchers misidentifying Great-bills as Grey Herons, a northern bird that has been recorded only twice in Australia, and therefore a very desirable 'tick'.

WHITE-NECKED HERON

At Bladensburg, we camped next to a dry creek-bed with a few small ponds of water trapped by rock. Early one morning, Peter went to investigate some nearby spinifex, and I headed up the creek. From a distance, I could see a heron stalking and fishing in a small pond. As I gradually crept closer, I could see it was catching plenty to eat – small fish and crustaceans no longer than a little finger. When I was within six metres, I slowly sat down, soaking up the sunshine after a night below zero. The heron continued to fish and, for 45 minutes, was joined by a Willie Wagtail that flitted over the water's surface, snapping at insects the big bird had disturbed. Over the next few hours, many birds came in to drink – Magpie-larks, bronzewings, Crested Pigeons and Galahs. Around midday the heron became wary, watching the sky, then took off suddenly, followed by the wagtail. A buzzard flew over, the pond was left to the fish, and I headed back to camp for lunch. Ah! I do enjoy this.

WHITE-FACED HERON

All egrets are herons but not all herons are egrets. Basically an egret is a white heron, but several, such as the Eastern Reef and Western Reef Egrets, have dark morphs. They are classified together in the genus *Egretta*. The reason I mention it is because the White-faced Heron is included in *Egretta,* so perhaps should be regarded as the White-faced Egret. I suspect it once had a white morph as well, which was probably not suited to Australian conditions, so gradually disappeared. On our travels through the interior we often come across White-faced Herons but nowhere nearly as frequently as the larger White-necked. I can't recall seeing either on salt lakes or salty streams, so I was surprised when Raoul showed me his pictures of a heron elegantly striding through the surf on a stormy day (above).

LARGE WATERBIRDS

On Lake Toolibin, WA, Ray Garstone and I found a nesting colony of Nankeen Night-Herons near a colony of Eastern Great Egrets; there was also a Yellow-billed Spoonbill (above) nesting nearby. We set up a number of hides where I spent magical days watching and photographing. I was surprised to see the night-heron (left) feeding its chicks during the day, as it normally hunts for food at night. I was operating my large-format camera at the time and was so excited that I forgot to remove the dark slide. So I have a dozen sheets of unexposed film to prove that night-herons sometimes feed their offspring during daylight hours. We built a hide in a swamp sheoak about 30 metres from the egrets so we could watch proceedings. When I checked a fortnight later three pairs of egrets had built their nests in the tree next to the hide. So I gratefully obliged (right).

AUSTRALIAN PELICAN

Once they become airborne, pelicans are masters of the air, catching thermals and soaring aloft until almost out of sight. Then a shallow dive to the next thermal, where they spiral aloft again and so on, covering long distances with little effort. From that great height their horizons are vastly extended, so it is no surprise that they should arrive at fish-rich waterways far inland in good years. We camped one wet year on Eyre Creek in the Simpson Desert with a dozen or more pelicans for company and watched them fishing. Each seemed to be rather possessive of its small section of the creek and we witnessed numerous aggressive interactions (above). More interesting to us, though, was the effort expended in trying to dispossess cormorants and darters of their hard-won booty. Most of the fish caught by the Little Black Cormorants were small eel-tailed catfish and hardly worth the energy put into the usually unsuccessful attempts at piracy. The cormorants would dive but had to come up again because they are unable to swallow their catch underwater. The only way they could escape the harassment was to swim a long way underwater before surfacing.

AUSTRALIAN PELICAN

It seems strange to watch pelicans like these on the beaches close to home, then later find perhaps the same birds out in the desert, even as far as Kati Thanda (Lake Eyre). How do they know when to head inland? It would be most counterproductive to arrive in a dry year, so they must have an in-built meteorological weather station. Flocks gather, take off and a month later are breeding in large colonies. Then it's back to badger fishermen on the beaches.

LITTLE BLACK CORMORANT

This cormorant was not swimming in a river of blood, but in the reflection of canyon walls in the Macdonnell Ranges, central Australia. Although it was solitary, it was in breeding condition, evidenced by the white spots scattered over the head. After spending time in the water fishing, cormorants emerge on to a rock or tree branch and spread out their wings to dry.

PIED CORMORANTS

Equally at home on offshore islands, estuaries, inland lakes, rivers and streams, the Pied Cormorant has no trouble finding fish in water clear or opaque. In the breeding season the colour of the facial skin brightens and is used in courtship displays. After breeding is completed the facial skin loses a lot of its colour (left and above). These two birds were on Eyre Creek feeding on eel-tailed catfish. The Little Pied Cormorant is much more partial to fresh water, particularly swamps surrounded by melaleauca thickets, where they breed. Nests we examined after the breeding season were covered in round 'buttons', the only remains of the fresh-water crayfish the chicks were fed on. We came across the bird on the right accompanying a Little Black Cormorant in one of the gorges in the Macdonnell Ranges. We have come across both species nesting in the same colony.

beware little fish!
on cookawinchica creek:
gull-billed terns hunting

GULL-BILLED TERN

Where the inland creeks and streams cross roadways there is often a causeway. When the water flow slows to a trickle, fish moving upstream to spawn can't proceed further and accumulate in large numbers downstream from the causeway, attracting cormorants, darters, pelicans and terns. We remember some of our best days' birding at Cuttaburra crossing and Cookawinchica Creek near Bedourie, Qld, watching three species of terns exploiting the boil of eel-tailed catfish. The Gull-billed Terns were the most common, nearly all in non-breeding plumage with the crown white and the ear-patch black. Sometimes they went into the water with a big splash, like the bird in breeding plumage on the right; at other times they neatly plucked a fish from the surface with scarcely a ripple (left); the fish it missed is just visible. The tern in Sally's shot above lost its grip on the slippery fish but recovered it before it hit the water.

GULL-BILLED TERNS

CASPIAN TERN

I first photographed the Caspian Tern in 1962 (left), at its nest on the Lacepede Islands, about 100 km off the Kimberley coast. In those days I had to conserve film, so only took two or three pictures. Fifty years later using a digital camera we couldn't resist taking several hundred shots of the Caspians fishing for eel-tailed catfish on Eyre Creek in the Simpson Desert (above and right). As can be seen the water in the creek was quite muddy, almost opaque, yet these and other terns had no trouble sighting and catching fish. Many of the adults were loudly pursued by young terns hoping for a feed, so they had obviously bred somewhere nearby, probably on a sandy lacustrine island.

GULLS

The Silver Gull (above) and the much larger Pacific Gull (left) are resident species; I'm not so sure whether the Kelp Gull (right) has been breeding here long enough to be considered an Australian bird. First recorded in WA in 1924, probably as a straggler from a population in South Africa, it wasn't detected breeding until 1958, most likely involving birds from New Zealand. Since then it has become established here, part of an expansion in many parts of the southern hemisphere. The individual Sally photographed in Tasmania (right) had a dark eye like a South African bird rather than the yellow eye one would expect from New Zealand imports. That gulls can travel widely is evidenced by the fact that eight vagrant species have been recorded on our shores. They are able to travel over oceans because they can feed as they go, can rest on the water if they get tired and can drink salt water (as the two gulls pictured to the left are doing). Excess salt is excreted through a pair of nasal glands attached to the eye sockets.

AUSTRALASIAN GREBE

Grebes have small wings and would appear to be clumsy fliers, yet they manage to find their way to isolated ponds in the most unlikely places, probably by flying at night and detecting the glint of water as they pass by. When I lived in a small railway siding on the Nullarbor Plain, grebes occasionally landed on the silver roofs at night, mistaking them for water. These pictures exemplify this small grebe's ability to turn up wherever there are expanses of freshwater anywhere in Australia. On an ephemeral clay-pan in western Queensland we found a number of pairs nesting in the Wavy Marshwort. We often visit the area and in 40 years have only seen the clay-pan filled twice (left and above). At Ormiston Gorge in the Macdonnell Ranges, central Australia, (right) we noticed two grebes, one adult and the other immature. Sally in particular was enchanted with the spectacle of one or the other floating on the magical reflections of the gorge's walls. These walls overhang the waterhole to such an extent that we pondered the question of how the grebes got there, or indeed if they would be able to fly out, without reaching a reasonable conclusion.

LARGE BUSH BIRDS: *NON-PASSERINES*

Brown Falcon.

About half of the world's birds are non-passerines. Whereas all passerines are more-or-less related to each other to varying degrees, each of the 22 groups (orders) of non-passerines found in Australia is unrelated to the others. Some, such as emus, ducks, pigeons and seabirds, have a very long evolutionary history and were already well developed before Australia broke away from Antarctica. Now non-passerines occupy all habitats from oceans to deserts. The majority are resident but some, like shorebirds, some kingfishers and cuckoos, are summer migrants, while many seabirds arrive in winter. Some of the bush birds are very large, like emus and bustards; others, like button-quail, are quite small, but all are much bigger than the smallest passerines.

EMU

In 1865 John Gould drew attention to the slaughter of Emus in Tasmania, writing: "How much will the loss of this fine bird be regretted by every right-minded person who claims Tasmania as his fatherland?' The warning was not heeded and the Tasmanian Emu is no more: neither are the Kangaroo Island and King Island Emus. Of the mainland Emus, Gould warned "Further and further back, however, will it be driven until it be extirpated, unless some law be instituted to check its wanton destruction.' Luckily laws have been passed for the protection of all vertebrate wildlife, and Emus have benefited, being regularly sighted in numbers on any trip through the outback, like those we saw (left) on a dusty day in the Simpson Desert.

AUSTRALIAN BUSTARD

Bustards seem to us to have a supercilious air, due to the way they appear to 'look down their noses' (left). In fact, their eyes are positioned so that they can stare forwards under the beak. They look very similar to the African Kori Bustard and at one time were thought to be the same species. However, when I saw Kori in the Emirates I could see the difference; it is a much bigger bird. HRH Sheik Sultan bin Zayed Al Naryan, who breeds them for conservation, gave Pat a primary feather which I would guess is the biggest of any bird. The Australian Bustard is a strong flier, but I have never seen one higher than 50 metres above the ground, and I doubt if they are capable of soaring. The birds on the right were feasting on a Spur-throated Locust plague on the flood plains of the Diamentina River. On the left is a solitary female caught in a sudden rain storm in the Simpson Desert.

WEDGE-TAILED EAGLE

Until 1970 the Wedge-tailed Eagle was subject to massive persecution, with more than 30,000 killed each year in the mistaken belief it was responsible for lamb mortality. A study by CSIRO Wildlife Division exonerated it and numbers have recovered except in Tasmania, where the population of the subspecies *fleayi* is now so low its long-term survival is in some doubt. On the mainland it is frequently encountered while feeding on road kill – most of the birds observed are young ones like these two. We keep a record of all the raptors we see from the car on our travels; the wedge-tail is the sixth most common sighted, with one every 160.4 km. The bird on the left with a full crop is probably about 15 months old, judging from its wing moult; the innermost primary has been moulted and regrown. The bird on the right is threatening a raven, which we have snapped in the act of jumping backwards after it came too close, trying to steal a morsel of kangaroo meat.

LITTLE EAGLE

On our travels we see Little Eagles from the car much less frequently than the Wedge-tailed, one for every 1,505.6 km travelled The low numbers are probably a reflection of the fact that they rarely feed on road-side kills; we have only seen one, a dark-morph bird, on a dead kangaroo (above) near Tambo, Qld. However, we do find their nests regularly. On the right is a pale-morph bird; they are much more common than the dark morph. These eagles are well-named, being quite small, but they are very efficient hunters; we have seen them take crows and corellas in flight, as well as rabbits and reptiles up to the size of the Sand Monitor on the ground. At nests where we watched from hides, fast-flying birds like Australian Ringnecks, Elegant Parrots and Tree Martins were provided by the males, as well as rabbits – this diversity is a tribute to their hunting ability.

SMALL KITES

Australia is rich in rodents, with about 60 species in all, including several that have been introduced. Two raptors in particular rely on them as principal items of prey. Both hover expertly, searching the ground below for their elusive quarry. The Letter-winged Kite (left and above) is associated with the Long-haired Rat which inhabits the Channel Country of Qld, NSW and SA, extending to the Barkly Tableland in the Northern Territory. To prey on the rat, this kite has developed nocturnal habits and has very large eyes. The Black-shouldered Kite (right), shown here with a Swamp Rat, hunts during daylight hours but well into the evenings. Its main prey nowadays appears to be the introduced House Mouse that has spread widely across the continent.

SPOTTED HARRIER

Everyone's idea of beauty is different, so it is unlikely that any survey to find Australia's most beautiful bird would arrive at a consensus of opinion. I would cast my vote for the Spotted Harrier. I love its soft polka-dotted plumage, and the way it flies so elegantly and effortlessly. I vividly remember the first one I saw, floating over saltbush and bluebush near Kalgoorlie when I was about 14 years old. It so impressed me that I wrote a brief note that was published in the *Kalgoorlie Miner*, my first venture into print. The adult (left and right) is quite unmistakeable, but the juvenile (above) is rather similar to some other raptors. One specimen from the Kimberley was even described as a race of the Swamp Harrier. In other parts of the world there are a number of species of harriers. All nest on the ground either in long grasses or reeds. The Spotted is the only one that consistently nests in trees, although a few individuals of one European species have recently been recorded doing so, probably as a result of pressure by introduced predators.

WHISTLING KITE

It is quite surprising how often the call of the Whistling Kite is heard in the background of older Hollywood movies set in Amazonian and African jungles, far, far from home. It is a stirring martial sound, one of the most typical cries of the Australian bush, suggestive of belligerence and aggression. So it is perhaps a minor disappointment to find that a lot of its food consists of carrion, although it is an expert fisher, snatching up surface-swimming fish on the run. The kite on the right was catching fish at Ormiston Gorge. Whistlers also don't mind harassing other birds to dispossess them of their legitimate quarry. Several times at the Lake Toolibin egret colony I have seen kites strike egrets on the back, presumably to force them to regurgitate their fish.

BROWN FALCON

Wherever we travel in inland areas, except for the most extreme gibber plains, we find Brown Falcons, one for every 138.8 km of road driven. They choose prominent perches from which they locate their preferred prey of reptiles, small mammals and grasshoppers, so are easy to spot. They have longer legs than other falcons, possibly an adaptation to reptile quarry. One I watched capturing a snake surprised me with the distance it was able to stretch out one leg to grasp the reptile's head while keeping out of striking distance. I suspect its legs will become longer and longer with time, finishing up something like the reptile-specialist Secretarybird from Africa. The male on the left is cleaning its beak; the female on the right is not calling but yawning, relaxed with one foot up, totally bored with us watching from ten metres away. Brown Falcons are variable in colour, ranging from pale cinnamon to very dark brown; above is a dark-plumaged bird from near Eulo, Qld.

OWLS

My friend Grant was harvesting his wheat crop at Gulugaba, Qld, when an Eastern Grass Owl flew out ahead of the tractor. I imagine 99 per cent of farmers wouldn't have known what it was but Grant did and immediately swerved. To his relief, when he ran back and checked, he found he had just missed a nest containing eggs and small chicks. He left a swathe of wheat, hoping for the best, and contacted me. I drove out to the farm where we saw that the nest was exposed to sunlight, so not knowing what else to do we placed a box shelter for protection and hoped the adult would return. When we checked next day the eggs and chicks had been moved about five metres into the protection of the narrow swathe Grant had left. I can imagine the owl carrying the chicks in its beak, but it must have rolled the eggs across the ground. Over a period of days we moved a hide up to within ten metres and obtained a series of photos at night with a long lens (left). The grass owl is one of the barn owl mob, characterised by the flat facial disc and asymmetrical ear-holes; they hunt as much by sound as by sight. The Powerful Owl (right) feeds principally on possums and is the largest of the hawk owl group, substantially bigger and heavier than any of our four barn owl species.

FROGMOUTH AND OWLET-NIGHTJAR

Active at night, frogmouths spend daylight hours perched in trees whose bark their plumage closely matches. If disturbed, instead of flying away they elongate their bodies, beak stretched skyward, mimicking dead branches. When relaxed, such as the bird sunning itself (far right), they have a very different profile. On the far right is the widespread Tawny Frogmouth of the more humid areas; the bird to the near right is the form inhabiting the the arid interior. The Australian Owlet-nightjar is quite vocal, even during daylight hours, making it easy to locate, particularly when sunning itself at the entrance to its daytime roost (above).

DIAMOND DOVE

When we lived in Derby, WA, in the 1960s we often kept watch at a small bore which overflowed into a pond that attracted finches and doves and incidentally the first recorded Eastern Yellow Wagtail. By far the most numerous were the hundreds of Diamond Doves that came in to drink. A pair of sparrowhawks also kept watch there: they probably caught one dove each per day for most of the year, increasing their catch to five daily while they were feeding chicks, accounting for about 1,000 annually. However we witnessed many unsuccessful attacks which we thought were due to a 'whistle-tip' in the doves' wings; the last centimetre of the outer primary on each wing is narrow and emits a distinct whistle when the bird takes off, which is no doubt disconcerting to predators as well as a warning to other doves. Add to that the flash of white in the outer tail-feathers causing misdirection and there is a good chance of escape.

CRESTED PIGEON

The 'whistle tip' in the wing of the Crested Pigeon (below) is on the third primary from the outer-edge; it makes a very loud noise and is probably exaggerated by the powerful wing-beats. We feel that the Crested is close to aerodynamically perfect because of the way it can glide for considerable distances after a few wing-beats. Perhaps aircraft engineers should take a look at its wing design. Anyway, it is very efficient in many ways and appears to have benefited from the environmental impacts of humans. No doubt Crested Pigeons imagine that the sole function of humans is to provide them with ideal conditions for living and breeding. In the year 2150 I regretfully predict that the list of Australian birds will be limited to sparrows, Indian Mynas, Fairy Martins, Silver Gulls, Australian White Ibises, crows and Crested Pigeons, and perhaps Galahs and Budgerigars for colour. For the moment, the individual on the left was drinking at sundown on Cooper Creek, and on the right is a bird that pretty much owns our backyard.

FLOCK BRONZEWING

Huge flocks were reported throughout inland Australia until the early part of the 20th century when, mysteriously, this formerly abundant pigeon seemed to disappear for many years. Now the flocks have recovered, if not in their former numbers, still in impressive and spectacular congregations. These photographs were taken by us on Eyre Creek in the Simpson Desert, western Queensland. We sat hidden in the lignum each evening to watch the soul-soaring sight of the bronzewings coming to drink. They habitually made a circuit or two in tightly packed formation to check all was clear then crashed down at the water's edge to take a few hasty sips before hustling on their way. Several hundred would land, drink and depart in the space of a minute or two. They fly so fast that one would think nothing could catch them, but we saw here and elsewhere Black Falcons overtaking them.

SPINIFEX PIGEON

True desert-dwellers, these little pigeons remind us of clockwork toys as they hustle about in spinifex among the rocks. In central Australia (above) they are redder than birds at the eastern edge of their range (left and right). When disturbed they take off with a loud whistle and share the Crested Pigeon's aerodynamic perfection with the ability to glide for long distances after a few vigorous flaps. Near one of our camps close to a waterhole in the desert we were surrounded by dozens of these pigeons, which attracted a goshawk. Over three days we saw the hawk make numerous unsuccessful attempts to catch one. We are sure it didn't feed in the time we were there, and on the fourth day it soared to great height and headed off to try somewhere else. On the other hand a sparrowhawk arrived, caught one on its first attempt and, heavily burdened, carried the victim away.

BROWN CUCKOO-DOVE

One would think, given the name 'cuckoo-dove', that these birds are parasitic, laying their eggs in the nests of other pigeons and doves, but the name derives from some fancied resemblance to cuckoos. I can't detect much similarity; perhaps immature ones (right) have barring vaguely reminiscent of some female cuckoos in 'hepatic' plumage. In flight they are more cuckoo-like but have rounded rather than pointed wings, and tails that are considerably broader. What attracts our attention are: the eyes, a startling combination of red and blue; the subtle iridescence on the neck; and the way what appears to be a small, neat beak expands to an enormous gape when it feeds on fruits like the Tobacco Bush. The cuckoo-dove is one of the main propagators of this poisonous weed, which can cause fatalities in humans if consumed, but does not affect the doves, or figbirds, at all. They often eat the fruit before it turns yellow when toxicity levels are highest.

KINGFISHERS

These are also known as 'forest kingfishers,' although of the three only the Sacred Kingfisher inhabits open forests – it is more common in woodlands. A female is shown (left) perched at a nesting burrow dug into an arboreal termite mound. Right is a Collared Kingfisher, a widespread species that is confined to mangroves. On the far right is a Red-backed Kingfisher, which is more at home throughout the arid interior, coming to its nest-hole in a terrestrial termite mound. To take the photo I sat in a hide near Derby, WA, throughout a very hot November day – the kingfishers arrived with lizards or grasshoppers every 20 to 40 minutes. When my wife came to get me out of the hide I was so baked that I was delirious; she later claimed I got into the back seat of the car and said "Someone's pinched the steering wheel."

desert kingfisher
thinks because they both have scales
that lizards are fish

streaming trail of light
searching for paradise lost:
rainforest comet

KINGFISHERS

The Buff-breasted Paradise-Kingfisher (left) was responsible for me uprooting my family from Western Australia and moving to Queensland to live. On the evidence of H C Richter's lithograph in Gould's *Birds of Australia* I considered it to be one of our most beautiful birds. So when I read an account by Mrs Billie Gill of her observations in the rainforest near her home, I decided to head for Innisfail. Billie showed me some nests in small termite mounds and I set up a hide to try for pictures. I soon found that high humidity and torrential rain are not the best conditions in which to be operating potentially lethal electronic flash equipment. I hadn't realised how dark rainforests are – the lighting in most published photos I had seen was overcompensated by the camera's light-meter so that everything looked bright and green. The reality is quite different. So the flash was necessary to light my subject and to provide an exposure of 1/5000th of a second to freeze the bird's flight. As well I was operating a huge 5x4 camera with bellows extending about 60 cm. The leather bellows grew mould, the lens kept fogging up and the flash kept shorting with a sound like a .303 rifle firing. So in a week or so in the hide I shed a lot of weight and only managed half a dozen pictures. Do I make it sound difficult? I enjoyed every minute watching Richter's painting come to life. On the right is a Forest Kingfisher. It too nests in termitaria, but invariably in those that build on tree trunks.

LAUGHING KOOKABURRA

The kookaburra is everyone's favourite due to its laughing call and its ready acceptance of hand-outs in the backyard. But I had my doubts as a youngster in Western Australia; it is not a native of the west but was introduced by Colonel Le Souef, director of the South Perth Zoo and father of my biology teacher. It quickly spread throughout the south-west, and there was a school of thought that suggested it might be preying on nestling birds. To test this theory I searched for a nest in an area with many nesting birds and found an ideal site in the Woodanilling golf

course. The nest-hole was in an old Wandoo; within a hundred metres were about a dozen clearly visible nesting birds. So I set up a hide and waited in anticipation. Every 20 minutes one of the adults arrived with a succulent morsel. Guess what. No nestling birds, only grasshoppers and reptiles, including skinks, dragons and a metre long Dugite, which was still writhing. I managed a shot of it, at that time probably the only photograph of a kookaburra with a snake it had actually killed itself, and my best ever picture, lost alas by a publisher. Vindicated in my mind as a bird predator, but to herpetologists?

RAINBOW BEE-EATER

When a bee-eater catches a bee in flight it returns to its perch; before swallowing the victim, it is wiped on the branch to remove the sting. At the dozen or so nest-burrows we have watched, nearly all of the insects carried in for the chicks consisted of dragonflies, cicadas and wasps, but there were very few bees. I found my first bee-eater tunnel in Kalgoorlie, where I was the only boy in the history of the town never to go looking for gold, preferring birds.

*rainbow bee-eaters
in the bush near kalgoorlie
digging deep for gold*

QUAIL

Brown Quail are abundant in my grassy back-paddock but they keep so well-hidden that I rarely see them. The only places I have photographed them are far from home: Cuttaburra Crossing near Bedourie, Qld, (right), the south-west, the tip of Cape York and the Kimberley. I only need to get a shot in Tassie and I'll have one from each of the four corners and one from the middle. The bird on the left was a Stubble Quail I saw in Neville Beeck's paddocks in 1964 near Katanning, WA. Neville was a very keen conservationist and was passionate about banding birds. We were often co-opted to race around his stubble fields at night waving spotlights and nets, hoping to catch and band quail. Some nights we caught more than a hundred but in all the time we assisted we never caught a banded bird so there must have been a steady stream of hundreds of quail passing through Neville's property. Neville and Dorothy Beeck invited Pat and me to join them on a trip to Thevenard Island off the north-west coast, a good birding site. They did warn us that there was an aboriginal fertility stone on the island. We managed some great shots of Ospreys and Fairy Terns, but guess what? We added another photographer to the world nine months later.

SOUTHERN STONE-CURLEW

My father, a clergyman, told me when we were living in Kalgoorlie about an aboriginal woman whose children had been taken away. She said to him she could hear them crying at night. Many many years later I was listening to our resident stone-curlews calling sadly in the back-paddock and the story came into my mind with a poem ready-formed. Stone-curlews are common in the outer suburbs of Brisbane where I live but these photos were taken on Mrs Grieves' property in densely populated Kenmore. She was very proud of them and rang me often with the latest news, sometimes reporting tragedies inflicted by dogs. On one occasion she found one paralysed; I took it home for examination and found a tick that I carefully removed. Within two hours it had recovered and was taken back and released. As far as I know it is still there, crying in the night.

sad wongaii woman
hears the cries of lost children:
stone-curlews wailing

BANDED LAPWING

I have two childhood memories of Banded Lapwings at Manjimup, WA. The first is their calls, evocative of loneliness and melancholy, as they flew over at night as I lay snuggled in my eiderdown (made from real eider feathers). The other, when I was a bit older, concerned a nesting pair that dive-bombed my friends and me as we snuck into a paddock to pinch turnips. The bolder of us repeatedly dared the plovers to attack and we would then turn tail and run. Unfortunately the noise attracted the attention of the farmer who, annoyed at our previous forays into the turnip field, came out waving his gun and peppered us with saltpetre as we climbed through the fence. Why we raided that turnip field I do not know; we hated turnips. I still do. One good year in the desert we came across many Banded Plovers breeding, including this pair on a treeless swale between sand-hills. We used the car as a hide since they were used to seeing vehicles driving past and thus paid no heed. Their three small chicks were running about pecking at the ground and pretending to feed. As the youngsters tired, one by one, they ran to a parent and snuggled up in its skirts, looking like an eight-legged Jake-the-peg (left). Above is the other adult brooding the three chicks at the nest site.

INLAND DOTTEREL

Like the desert quail-thrushes, Inland Dotterels prefer stony ground in central Australia. If disturbed they often turn their backs and stand still, their colour and pattern making them quite difficult to spot on the vast rock-strewn plains (above). If the observer persists they tend to run rather than fly, taking to the wing as a last resort. They nest on the ground; if an incubating bird has to leave the eggs it will cover them with surrounding debris, something we have not witnessed ourselves.

CUCKOOS

When I was about six or seven years old I was given a book about British birds, so I knew more about Lesser Whitethroats, Dartford Warblers and Eurasian Cuckoos than I did about our local birds. When I saw a cuckoo chick being fed by fairy-wrens I didn't tell anyone because I thought they wouldn't believe that I had seen a British bird in Australia. But there are far more cuckoos in Australia, so many that it has been postulated that co-operative breeding in birds like fairy-wrens evolved because a group is more likely to defend a nest successfully than a pair. Usually the Pallid Cuckoo parasitises larger passerines with cup-shaped nests, but I recall seeing a pair of spinebills, tiny by comparison, frantically trying to fill the crop of a chick in Western Australia. On the left is a female; the male is above. The Horsfield Bronze-Cuckoo is much smaller and parasitises small birds like fairy-wrens and thornbills, including the Chestnut-rumped Thornbill that nests in tree hollows.

MAJOR MITCHELL'S COCKATOO

Explorer Major Mitchell didn't discover this spectacular cockatoo, but he made a beautiful painting of it while travelling in the outback, included later in the published journal of his travels. He did discover Bourke's Parrot, though, so didn't entirely waste his time in the bush. Each time we head off westward we await with anticipation the first sighting of Major Mitchell's; then we know we are entering the good country, and the cares of civilisation fall behind...

Sally recalls: I was otherwise preoccupied but watching a small flock not far away; one couragous bird (left) decided to come and say hello, sitting a few meters above me. We had quite a friendly conversation as he studied me and kindly waited for me to adjust my attire so I could grab my camera and take his portrait. This was a week into my first desert trip, and since then I have felt an affectionate bond with such a beautiful and gentle parrot, wild and free.

GALAH

Galahs have proliferated since humans started growing wheat and other crops for them and providing water in otherwise waterless places for them to drink. As a consequence we have seen flocks numbering thousands and no doubt you have too. Spectacular as they wheel, flashing in an instant from grey to pink. These photos were taken at one of our favourite places on the Diamentina River at Birdsville. Most visitors to this famous outback town head for the even more famous pub, but we are attracted to a distinctly less-amber fluid. Each time we visit we are not disappointed and so it was on this occasion. As the sun sank hundreds of Galahs arrived to drink (right). A star-picket was a popular perch and there were many squabbles over possession. The picture on the left was taken in the last of the sun's rays; less than a minute later I took the next shot (above) after the sun had sunk, for a very different effect.

GALAH

We keep an eye on the weather in the arid inland and if heavy rain has fallen give it a while for things to start happening then head out. Thus we came across this waterhole and set up camp. I spied a goshawk so set off and followed it at a distance, arriving back after sunset. Sally said she had seen an amazing thing: Galahs drinking on the wing. I hadn't heard of such a thing and her photos were intriguing, so next evening we sat waiting for the Galahs to arrive. They came in small groups of 20 to 40 birds, mostly from the north-east. Soon there were hundreds in the surrounding trees, then one after the other the boldest flew down to skim over the surface, reaching down to take a sip. Incredible! Protruding from the water were rocks that quickly became covered by thirsty Galahs and corellas, imbibing fluid in the normal way. But dozens continued to drink on the wing, even though it required considerably more effort than drinking at the water's edge. The light was low so we had to increase the camera ISO to 2400 and beyond to have a hope of capturing the action. On returning home we went through our library without finding any references to similar activity, although I can't imagine we are the only observers to have witnessed what may be a survival strategy in areas such as this with raptors on the prowl. We saw Peregrine and Black Falcons, hobbies, goshawks and a sparrowhawk there.

BUDGERIGAR

Very much a 'boom-or-bust' bird, the Budgerigar breeds up in the interior in times of plenty and dwindles in numbers in drought years. I remember walking along a creek in the Macdonnell Ranges after a very wet season in the 1970s and the sound of budgies was so loud we couldn't hear ourselves talk. Every knot-hole in the River Red Gums was occupied; a lot of the noise was made by young birds begging for food at the entrance to their nest-holes. For as long as food lasts many budgies will continue breeding, In the west I once found two nests in close proximity, each containing a female on eggs being fed by the same male; on the right, a female is soliciting food from her mate. Assuming the females bred three times that year, the male probably sired more than two dozen chicks. After breeding large flocks congregate, and if conditions deteriorate they will travel looking for food, turning up far from their normal habitat.

232

AUSTRALIAN RINGNECK

The ringneck occupies much of the southern two-thirds of Australia; but in times past some populations became isolated due to natural phenomena such as ice ages. In isolation these populations developed plumage patterns to suit the changing environment, on the way to becoming new species. When conditions improved the populations spread out, coming into contact with others. As they had not fully assumed specific status they hybridised along the zones of contact, so they are now regarded as subspecies, although in the past they were considered to be separate species. These photos illustrate some of the various forms: far left, the bird formerly known as the Port Lincoln Parrot, feeding on Ruby Saltbush, Alice Springs, NT; left, the bird once known as the Mallee Ringneck, feeding on Eremophila blossoms, Tambo, Qld; above right, an example of the Cloncurry Parrot, gleaning lerps from eucalypt leaves, Camooweal, Qld; and below right a hybrid between the Port Lincoln Parrot and the Mallee Ringneck, eating berries, Mt Chambers, SA.

VARIED LORIKEET

I found some Varied Lorikeets near Derby, WA, roosting each night in a eucalypt tree-hollow, so made a hide on a nearby branch 70 feet up, and sat each day at sunset while they noisily returned. One evening I arrived to find the branch I'd been sitting on lying on the ground. Hmm. It could just as easily have fallen while I was sitting on it – just one of many lucky escapes. Anyway, I still love Varied Lorikeets but the one above insisted on having the last word.

The Photographs

When I took my first colour photographs in 1950 a roll of Kodachrome cost one third of my weekly wage so, like every one else, I was very careful to try and get the exposure, lighting and composition right. When a film was finished it was sent off to Kodak in a small canister and a self-addressed bag. Great excitement a fortnight later when the transparencies arrived back, then the inevitable disappointment when each was held up to the light; why didn't I do this or why didn't I do that? The usual fault was the exposure, either too dark or too light; if it wasn't correct there was no way to fix it. If the problem wasn't exposure it was usually focusing. At that time the cameras didn't have a built-in light meter and had to be focused manually, so taking a good picture was pretty much hit and miss. Unless one was deficient in self-criticism or aesthetic sense, the best thing to do was throw the duds away. Compare that to today's digital cameras: the number of shots you can take on a chip is unlimited, and once it is full it can be downloaded onto the computer and wiped clear so you can continue shooting (we sometimes take a thousand or more shots a day and download at night, deleting any where the bird has flown or is in a poor position). The sensitivity can be altered from one shot to the next to suit the conditions, ISO 100 if the conditions are very bright to ISO 6400 and beyond when it is dark or you want a faster shutter speed; the camera basically sets the exposure, stabilises and focuses the lens. Best of all, though, there are remedies to rescue shots where the camera/photographer partnership fouled up by getting the exposure or focusing wrong (which happens often when trying to capture a fleeting glimpse).

Going through the pictures downloaded onto the computer, it soon becomes apparent to the photographer that very rarely is a shot exactly right, so it becomes necessary to use a programme such as Photoshop to 'correct' it. In the old days of colour film what you took was what you got. Not any more. Practically every shot you see taken with a digital camera has been manipulated in some way, a little or a lot – it can be sharpened, colour-corrected, enhanced; offending intrusions like blades of grass can be removed, skies can be lightened or darkened, shadows can be softened. So how can you as a viewer be secure in believing that each picture is a truthful representation? And does it need to be a 'truthful representation'? An 'artist' is not constrained by anything but the limits of imagination and many use photographs as a starting point. I would go so far as to say that some of the most exciting artists working today are those manipulating photographs to an unbelievable extent so that the end result is nothing like the image they started with. However, I believe there is an expectation in wildlife photography, and of birds in particular, that the scene is the same as appeared on the ground-glass screen of the camera at the instant of exposure. To be entirely truthful one would need to use a 50mm lens at f8 because that combination sees the world in much the same way as a human eye does. But it is not practical to use such a short focal length – most decent bird photographs are taken with lenses between 300mm and 1200mm; the longer the lens the more the background is thrown out of focus, aesthetically pleasing but not at all the way the human eye sees it, and therefore not 'truthful'. If a photographer has any expertise with Photoshop it is rarely possible to determine the degree of manipulation, so the viewer has to rely on the belief that there are no changes to the *essential elements* of the picture. In these accompanying samples we show how we work on our photos so you can judge how much to believe.

The picture of the avocet was taken with a Linhof camera on a sheet of Ektachrome film measuring about 10x13 cm and was lit by two high-speed flash-heads. Because it was taken so long

ago, the film had faded with a colour cast. This was corrected during scanning on an Epson scanner using a colour-correction filter. In the original the background was under-exposed because the flash didn't extend far enough. In Photoshop I was able to equalise the lighting by using *Shadows/Highlights*. There were ugly black shadows caused by poorly-positioned flash-heads; they were eliminated by cloning appropriate parts of the background and super-imposing them over the shadows. The exposure was then adjusted in *Levels,* the colour was adjusted in *Selective Colour* and *Saturation*, the picture was cropped and finally the whole image was sharpened in *Smart Sharpen*. Only a handful of images in this book required this level of correction.

Below is a composite image of a Brown Falcon flying, taken in the Simpson Desert. We approached the bird as it sat on top of a bush, and as it took off I kept my finger firmly on the release button, allowing the built-in motor-drive to fire at about seven frames per second. The resultant images were then stitched together in Photoshop using *Photomerge*. This is a facility usually

employed in taking panoramic landscapes but it is also handy for birds in flight, allowing one to examine how the wings function. It requires a bit of common sense, keeping the camera level as the bird's flight path is followed and only works if part of each individual picture overlaps its neighbours.

One of the most frustrating things about photographing birds in the wild is the apparently wilful propensity of grass-stems and twigs to get in the way. Fortunately offending items can be removed using Photoshop, but with it comes an obligation not to alter the bird, so must be used with great sensitivity. When I took this picture of a Yellow-rumped Thornbill on the Birdsville Track, I was unaware that a twig had imposed itself in typical fashion, so snapped away merrily. Alas the bad news hit me when

the images were opened that night in the computer. I was able to clone feathers matching the obscured ones and superimpose them over the twig. While I was at it I took out a twig in the background. Why did I bother? The reason is I have had more difficulty photographing this species than any other small bird.

The Poems

Birds to me are feathered poems. I am entranced by Japanese poets like Basho and Issa whose short seventeen-syllable poems, known as haiku, encapsulate so much insight into nature and the human condition. Ideally a haiku doesn't have a gestation period but is conceived fully-formed, in three lines of five, seven and five syllables. In theory, such a poem arrives in the mind in seventeen thought-seconds, hence the number of syllables. Many haiku require contemplation from the reader, as hidden between the lines are layers of meaning. Just because a poem has seventeen syllables, though, it is not necessarily a haiku, something I am conscious of when one pops into my mind. So my efforts herein are offered as short verses, not haiku. Perhaps one might just qualify:

wild bugles blowing

dark shadows obsure the moon

black swans overhead

On one level it recounts a childhood memory of swans uttering their soft bugling calls as they flew over at night; on another the dark shadows are clouds of pollution from fossil-fuel burning, and the swans epitomise birds hastening to extinction. On a further level the bugles imply global conflict caused by religious fundamentalism or wars over diminishing water and oil supplies or just plain stupid human insanity, the dark shadows bombers unloading mutually-assured destruction. It is also about depression – work that one out.

Peter Slater

INDEX

Apostlebird 106-7
Australasian Grebe 172-3
Australasian Pipit 96-7
Australian Bustard 178-9
Australian Pelican 156-9
Australian Ringneck 232-3
Australian White Ibis 172-3
Banded Honeyeater 71
Banded Plover 218-9
Banded Stilt 147
Black Honeyeater 71, 77
Black-faced Woodswallow 102-3
Black-fronted Dotterel 140-1,143
Black-shouldered Kite 185
Black Swan 128-9
Black-tailed Treecreeper 50
Bowerbirds 109
Brown Cuckoo-Dove 204-5
Brown Falcon 174-5, 190-1
Brown Honeyeater 77
Brown Quail 215
Brown Treecreeper 51
Budgerigar 230-1
Buff-breasted Paradise-Kingfisher 208
Caspian Tern 168-9
Cinnamon Quail-thrush 92-3
Chestnut-breasted Mannikin 82-3
Chirruping Wedgebill 46
Collared Kingfisher 207
Crested Pigeon 198-9
Crimson Chat 36-7

Diamond Dove 196-7
Double-barred Finch 86-7
Dusky Grasswren 32-3
Dusky Moorhen 36-9
Eastern Grass Owl 192
Eastern Great Egret 155
Eastern Yellow Robin 42-3
Emmott's Fairy-wren 20-1
Emu 176-7
Fairy Martin 58-61
Fawn-breasted Bowerbird 123
Flock Bronzewing 200-1
Forest Kingfisher 209
Galah 226-9
Gibberbird 38-9
Golden-backed Honeyeater 74-5
Golden-headed Cisticola 80-1
Great Bowerbird 122
Great-billed Heron 148
Grey-fronted Honeyeater 73
Grey-headed Honeyeater 72
Ground Cuckoo-shrike 94-5
Gull-billed Tern 164-7
Hardhead 130-1
Horsfield's Bronze-Cuckoo 223
Inland Dotterel 220-1
Kalkadoon Grasswren 28-31
Kelp Gull 171
Laughing Kookaburra 210-11
Letter-winged Kite 184-5
Lewin's Honeyeater 64-6
Little Black Cormorant 160-1
Little Eagle 182-3

Little Friarbird 68-9
Little Pied Cormorant 163
Little Wattlebird 66-7
Magpie-lark 104
Major Mitchell's Cockatoo 224
Masked Woodswallow 100-1
Nankeen Night-Heron 194
Noisy Friarbird 68-9
Orange Chat 34-5
Owlet-nightjar 194
Pacific Black Duck 132-5
Pacific Gull 170
Painted Finch 87
Painted Honeyeater 70
Pallid Cuckoo 222-3
Pied Butcherbird 105
Pied Cormorant 162-3
Plum-headed Finch 87
Powerful Owl 143
Rainbow Bee-eater 212-3
Red-backed Fairy-wren 26-7
Red-backed Kingfisher 207
Red-browed Finch 87
Red-capped Plover 144-5
Red-capped Robin 40-4
Red-kneed Dotterel 142-3
Red-necked Avocet 146-7
Redthroat 46
Rufous Treecreeper 50
Rufous-banded Honeyeater 76
Sacred Kingfisher 206
Satin Bowerbird 124-5
Scarlet Honeyeater 62-3

Silver Gull 171
Southern Stone-curlew 216-7
Southern Whiteface 47
Spinifex Pigeon 202-3
Spotted Bowerbird 110-115
Spotted Harrier 186-7
Spotted Pardalote 90-1
Straw-necked Ibis 149
Striated Pardalote 88-9
Stubble Quail 214
Tawny Frogmouth 195
Tree Martin 56-7
Varied Lorikeet 234-5t
Varied Sittella 52-3
Variegated Fairy-wren 22-5
Wedge-tailed Eagle 180-1
Weebill 48-9
Welcome Swallow 55
Western Bowerbird 116-21
Whistling Kite 188-9
White-backed Swallow 54
White-browed Treecreeper 51
White-browed Woodswallow 98-9
White-faced Heron 152-3
White-necked Heron 150-1
White-plumed Honeyeater 70
White-winged Fairy-wren 18-9
Willie Wagtail 78-9
Yellow-billed Spoonbill 154
Yellow-rumped Thornbill 44-5
Yellow-spotted Honeyeater 65
Zebra Finch 84-5

All our trips have been an absolute pleasure for me. Peter's knowledge of birds and cameras, his unassuming nature and quiet humour make an excellent travelling companion. *Sally Elmer*

I very rarely come across anyone whose company I enjoy in the bush, mostly because I like to stand still for long periods while others want to move on. Sally is one of the few who share my approach. Plus she is a good cook, does more than her share of the driving, can dig a car out of a bog and can change a tyre. *Peter Slater*